foil

defining poetry 1985-2000
edited by nicholas johnson

etruscan

exhibition

etruscan

28 Fowlers Court, Fore Street
Buckfastleigh
South Devonshire TQ11 0AA

ISBN 1 901538 28 1 / 1 901 538 32 x (cased l.s.e.)

etruscan is a member of lollipop www.indigogroup.co.uk-llpp

Distributed in USA by
SPD, 1341 7th Street, Berkeley, California 94710 USA,
available in England from
Peter Riley (Books), 27 Sturton Street, Cambridge CB1 2QG
and in Australia from
Collected Works, 256 Flinders Street, Melbourne 3000

Central design by A.G. Greenock.
Typeset by R.W Palmer at *Tuff Talk Press,* Bath.
Printed by *Short Run Press,* Exeter.

TO GAEL TURNBULL AND ROY FISHER

contents

introduction

CERTIFICATES
THAT PURCHASE THE PAST EASILY
AND ON OUR OWN TERMS

Sell everything then hope for the best *Maurice Scully*

Foil is a collection of poetry and prose texts by 33 writers, who first made their art public between 1985 and 2000. These writers operate in capitals and cities, ordinary locations and out on the wild verges: Stromness, Dartington, Aberwystwyth. *Foil,* like an unclean wing-mirror, highlights the fragmentary social nature of their labour within three devolved – separate countries.

The anthology is usually a way of tidying things up, offering some last crumbs of the crust back to those that first baked it, to scavengers on the road who would gain sustenance by it. *Foil* represents changes in expectation of – and within – language; idioms up for grabs. A wide range of speech seized as birthright. Punned, sampled or appropriated, serpentine and spatial, hysteric or vitriolic: this poetry pays keen attention to sound and has a driving pulse rhythm.

This folio offers a disparate gathering, before the chance is gone and the trail evaporates, of a not yet extinguished mass. A generation of writers, performers, activists, mavericks and shadowy presences – many not previously anthologised – drawn from small press publications and extensions of those networks. The parameters, post-*New British Poetry* (PALADIN, 1988), were to locate a body of writing which barely grazed Iain Sinclair's *Conductors of Chaos* (PICADOR, 1996). The 20th Century's last invisible generation.

Those wishing to discover how language pitches against sound, should read *Folk Lore 1-25* by Tim Atkins and *Vale Royal* by Aidan Andrew Dun. It is 1995 and they both issue unusual debuts; one printed in Paris the other in Verona; an eerie, disembodied Shropshire *sci-fi*, and a Kings Cross epic composed in triads. They create social scenarios referencing the deep past but remain modern alchemists. Consider Peter Manson, his poetry rebuilding earlier (often found) texts, taking a crowbar and a scalpel to rhetoric. Or Alison Flett (publishing earlier as Alison Kermack), vital performer, phonetic writer since the early 90s, whose books *Writing like a bastard*, and *Restricted Vocabulary* were promoted in South

Queensferry and Glasgow by CLOCKTOWER & REBEL INC..

> *Foil.*   Change the title.
>
> Change it?
>
> "Always change." said Niall Quinn.

I propose no systematic groupings of this work around specific approaches to language, text and poetry; because it's preferable to disrupt notions of category. Categorisation by location fails also: as these writers frequently *move*: my notebook full of speculative addresses and name changes. The location of allegiances wouldn't pay off either, and I don't subscribe to the notion of community, nor do I believe that the full scope of the work here is known, or even relevant to most of the writers here. *Foil's* running order happily plays bodies of work against themselves, while loosely following the chronological trail of those writings (those personas, Gothic, nihilist or samizdat; gender-exploratory, punk shadow or *fin de siecle*) as they emerged.

Foil marks a threshold for exhibition @ etruscan, launching its new performance book series (see inside back cover). A mix of scenes by writers – some bored rigid by the tags 'alternative canons', 'post post-modernist' or 'linguistically innovative'; of exchanges sweeping across the academic flatlands of L-A-N-G-U-A-G-E poetry as business pack; some exhilarated by texts, sourced globally, or from their own doorstep: – old, new and refined histories. The media of sonic performance, installation, choreography, visual writing or photography informs a good chunk of the work here. *Makars* and sonic performers, body poets, artists who install their work, to be projected on walkmans. Some pioneer their own CDs or translate literature into booklets like *Typhon Dru, Personal Pong*, catalogue two decades of classroom-desk graffiti, or occupy the *South London Gallery*. They get blacklisted by the *South Bank*, yet exhibit in Russia, Yugoslavia as well as the Institution of Rot, Crouch End. Descriptions circulate on performances by Khaled Hakim, known as a confrontational club performer, who didn't care to publish his 'scripts'. Into the mix goes a singer of raga, Rajiv C.Krishnan, Aaron Williamson's unique performances, the web site of poet-sinologist John Cayley and the short-lived but deeply implicating collective *However introduced to the Soles*, it's quite a doorstep;- while the British Isles festers asleep on its field, or mines a narrow seam of indifference.

The more orthodox production and distribution afforded Aaron Williamson's *A Holythroat Symposium* and *Cathedral Lung* (Creation

Records offshoot) and the long overdue Gaelic/English edition of Meg Bateman's writings *Lightness/ Aotromachd agus dain eile* helped both writers in becoming widely disseminated in the fields of – respectively – performance art and Scottish/Gaelic poetry. Caroline Bergvall, publishing in such 'fiction' territories as 'Pulp Action' with *RUSH: a long way from H* is worth viewing in the context of the rave culture.

Inspired by glam and punk, industrial or dub: writers here formed bands, others recorded. Many *Foil* biographies show second or dual languages, childhoods and education outside England. Being at one remove from the standardised English education system is one of the few links between this non-community of writers. This generation does not directly continue the tethering to the albatross of its predecessors. Perhaps a 'non successive continuum' in not being referential to the writing and polemic of two previous generations also mirrors their differences. The bio-data entries in *Foil* are relevant to 2000 – and this editor has no desire to trawl up earlier incarnations of the lineup here, but some background is worth permission, to show how fluid margins can be.

The exhibition catalogue for *The Shamanism of Intent* (GOLDMARK, 1991) (edited by Iain Sinclair, whose writings and audacious public events were a catalyst for many writers here) gives an early view on Aaron Williamson's first publications. Debut recordings by Caroline Bergvall and her first book, composed in French are now collectors items. Khaled Hakim published while still 'babyfaced' in *Equofinality* in 1984. Jennifer Chalmers promoted readings at King's College in the 1970s, long before her poetry publically surfaced. Aidan A D began *Vale Royal* in 1973- and Adrian Clarke who co-edited *Floating Capital,* a valedictory look at an 80s London poetic, also took time to gestate his work.

Most writers here have only had pamphlets published, fugitively prepared, sometimes un dated and with no statement of origin. The punk ethos of staple and go. Card cover, a few sheets of paper, the institute's photocopier, bang out two dozen copies. No social group can absorb those print runs. Unlike the great lava flows of publication, broadcasts and readings during 1965-78, no wave of activity has emerged with equivalent zest, or decisiveness. This clogging of the waterways shows that the golden age of British poetry publishing (in terms of circulation) ended 25 years ago. It exemplifies how little poetic-culture exists whereas there once was the hope of one.

Among the productions that must now be regarded as defining the areas of poetry under survey here, which treat text as environment, matched by the book are *Vale Royal*, (a letter press edition with a two CD performance of the book, printed by Stamperia Valdonega). The square book treatment afforded *an oblique view of a room in movement* and *Éclat* by Caroline Bergvall, has become a recognisable stylistic device. *Making Tents* (1987) and *idir eatortha (1996)* by Catherine Walsh foreground her attention to spatial form. (Sadly, Walsh's work was not made available to this anthology). *Off Ardglas*, *Brancepeth Beck*, *Satyrs and Mephitic Angels*, *Safety Catch*, *The table leaks its object*, *Folklore 1-25*, *forword* and *However introduced to the Soles* all constitute books that define a continuation in unorthodox experiment, harnessed to resplendent grand narratives or subversive *petites histoires* and equally resistant to them. Chapbooks by Amery, Longmire, Macias or Tarlo markedly constitute visual objects.

A tradition continues to be sustained, whereby poets remain inadequately published, and undistributed. The business of selling gets transacted at an elm slowness with equal surety. 'Getting to read these hard-to-come by publications involves personal transactions, a declaration of interest. It is the reader, not the poet, who must make herself known' said Karlien van den Beukel. What always matters, it seems, is the *event*, the endorsement of the published and performed work, the gesture of the reading invitation, networking, proofreading by stealth: because it remains possible. Whispers, allegiances, rituals of class, hierarchy and erudition: a cottage industry hiving off a fertile cream for what often disappointingly shows itself to be one issue, before another writer is sired out to the galleys. This manages to obscure the reader's ever present optimism in the next book that really happens. Feral poets flock down to pools which are by then stagnant.

Acts of disruption in the (meta) language, syntax and expression of Rob MacKenzie, Nick Laight, Kevin Nolan or Shelby Matthews in their totality may be political, however I hesitate to see many of the writers here as overtly political. This may link to rejection of the compulsion to consider global politics, or a inability to accomplish this, even for writers fluent in other languages and cultures, but going deep into this book, however nihilist some of it appears (as it is meant to) you, the reader, can unearth a subtle and razor-sharp political focus.

Writers locate a space, singly and multipally for composition, performance rehearsal, gestation, rituals, for exhibition and catalogue preparation. Space pitched against the ducking and diving for money and housing, raising children, the reduction of living and performance space contributes to the *frenzy* of writing here. In a country of hyper-information that would dearly love to bleach all our brains, a fight for real performance and writing space engenders work. The questioning of utilization of landscape by Meg Bateman, drawn to the Isle of Skye who learned Gaelic as a non-native speaker, contrasts with Rob MacKenzie, raised on the isle of Lewis. MacKenzie uses Lallans Scots, Gaelic and English, in the latter utilising a register at ease with, and enlivening Cambridge poetics (where he was a research student). Harriet Tarlo's careful, slow, graphed writing in *Brancepeth Beck* – affirms the realization 'to know that place does not come free'. Helen Macdonald draws on Tudor glossaries through her dual practice as a falconry expert. The nervy, caffeine-fixed futurscope of Bergvall's *Of Matter and Motion* (1992) centres a space for writing. The registers change, letters get deleted, computer viruses stalk her 1999 text here, *FLÉSH*.

Contemporary essayists and publishers whose work contributes to the culture would include the essayists Ian Hunt at ALFRED DAVID EDITIONS and BOOK WORKS, and Lucy Sheerman (alongside Karlien van den Beukel at rempress). Eck Finlay has been an exemplary publisher at MORNING STAR. INVISIBLE BOOKS facilitate many adventurous projects.

Andrew Duncan's *Angel Exhaust* (1992-9) has championed a generous range of writers: a key source for emerging poets, and one of the very few editors to explore what this new generation might be. In the 90s the journals *Object Permanence*, *Parataxis* and *Talus* charted a substantial amount of emerging writing: journals sure of their constituents. All four have since closed.

The *futurscope* I propose is now yours for the enjoyment. I thank the poets for the work they've created, and for letting me near them with sly and shy questions, theories and suppositions. Bill Griffiths' question on the editing of an anthology seems pertinent here. 'What are the virtues required of an editor? Tact (an ability to cheat?) sincerity (an ability to lie?), and compromise (the ability to accept victory as defeat) would seem essential.' I thank the presses for giving permission to represent their own labours. I thank Adam Geary for helping me shape this project and now I thank its typographer and copy-editor R W Palmer. And I dedicate my work on *Foil* to two poets, to Gael Turnbull and Roy Fisher– their work set a standard many years ago; the resonances get deeper. I hope they're the first to enjoy this book.

Nicholas Johnson

aaron williamson

I was in a taxi ride with Hank Williams not long ago. . .

It began at the Penultimate Hotel, you know, the last one before the One, and I stood there in that hole of sin, screaming, kicking, soaked in gin and Hank Williams Senior stepped in talking about 'these days you can't wear your heart on your sleeve when society's wiping its nose all over your jacket'.

So I took a taxi ride with Hank Williams through the piss-wild broken night, through the desperation and the broken teeth of this Year of our Lord, Nineteen Jesus Slept.

As everyone must wear out a fool's set of tyres in their time.

Taxi! Stop. Door, get in. Could you please drive around for a while? I want to try and calm down.

And I once rode in a taxi cab with Hank Williams and anyone could smell the after-shave upon his breath, the next step into death as songs about the fall of man and woman kind slipped out, slid down, as he slumped in his seat; just one smashed heart and a shrivelled liver hanging from his back and rubbing a world he'd like to shave off.

And he kept yelling out the window about the taxi-meter time as being different from calendar time, about how finally, you're just a tip of a bit of crusty toothpaste being squirted along by god-size hands. You know? Hands across the stratosphere, taxi cabs in tubes. . .but I couldn't hear him.

And we both stared sullenly out the window and I began to hear the ants fucking, the moon suck sucking the earth-sick weeds towards it as fuses flashed behind my eyes and out of a new curved spine sprang glistening teeth!

And we lit this firing squad cigar.

It's a shit world! He's an heart leper said John the rat man who was driving, you know, Hank Williams is an heart leper, most his talent comes from having a heart wrapped up in chains, I mean as cold as the cold, cold snow; a stinkin' cheatin' heart that tells cold tales that tell on you. . .

And the doors began to pump in like meat being charred, sweat breaking out behind the chisel-featured suit of Hank Williams in another town, another show, and another radio sings 'Cry no more nor cry no less, just simply cry in the wilderness. . .'

As we pulled up to watch a couple in the road: Adam stuck a gun in Eve and Pulled the Universe, wiped it off, re-loaded, kissed goodbye to cheap psychology and made the crab-lice in his head foxtrot. . . Flump.

It was never Adam and Eve in any case, it was Adam and Steve said Hank as we drove on. . .

Past a supermarket selling epilepsy, one man walks in and asks for 'a strong sad sleep, I'll never get out of this world a wife.'

A tunnel appears, it seems to lead to the other side of town but doesn't, it goes deeper and down, Eve stuck her hand in my cunt and touched the tip of the pink squashed willyman, wiped a tear from its eye. . .

And Hank slumped deeper in his seat and sang 'I'm so lonesome that I could cry'

And I said to Hank Williams man, we've got to try and get back.

As the tunnel swerved and blew in light, where we all end up, where it all begins, in the gutter of the Penultimate Hotel.

We were jamming nub ends even in our arteries by the time we got there.

As the fan clubs scratched and snarled against the taxi begging 'sing it Hank, just sing once more and make it all o.k. just sing it Hank and make it all, make IT all go away. . .'

And unitedly we sang fuck you.

We were ladelling our blood, rolling our sleeves and ladelling the blood off using syringes, winding down the windows and squirting the citizens.

Until Hank stepped out, stepped down, lost inside the seethe and swarm of another town, another show, yeah,

I once rode in a taxi with Hank Williams not long ago. I had to pay the fare.

Existence has no exit
bulbed out on fuckout,
snapped out of exits
eviled out of I-head:
what am I even doing here?
– I found out at last;
I was an ex-It,
simply a do-nut hole torn out of the sky
through which the coming dawn
commuters form
convulsions of birds
goin'
think I'd scorch my wings??

– well I could die
just for opening my mouth
I mean speaking such shit
I mean be killed by Satan and
HIS sidekick
– I'm no buddah,
I'm a wanker:
Buddah can you spare me a dimension?
How clever. Wanker.
Or just a mention?
– upon the smooth floors of galaxies...

You see?
I have with me, at all times,
the magic words
with which to form a sentence
of death.
Of course, I can't SAY them,
they're not playthings
...I grew a flower that filled me
with tears;
feathers upon my teeth,
my nerves were sticking out HERE
far enough to form wings:
a pair of clipped and soiled
wings
that flap but never get me
in the air:

I do nothing,
I go nowhere,
I see no-one.

think I'd scorch my wings?

The streets are filled with lead
through streets of molten lead
I walk between the heads
that grow between the pavement cracks
HOLD BACK !
. . . I hear news of disaster from the East
news of disaster from the West
news of disaster from all over
bankruptcy disaster
mmm squeezyfish in a town centre
I hear brood devourers, crazy talkers
mouths agape for bread and germs
employing metal dragnaughts screaming
lonesome in their hell
for none would yet themselves be eaten

something needs to give
because
the streets I walk are little more
than museums of dis-ease
perfect piles of domicilities
packed with ghostly breath
and your breath is nothing less than that
nada nada NO-thing
and your dead are even less, far less
allergic to the nub, Naomi we sup and retch
and sup and retch
here are the first the last us final reluctant
centurions
strangest kind of swarm
wives molesters rats and butterflies
mutually wounded
we can each ALGEBRAICALLY
make gears of progess SMART
smart on smarty
quite astonishing
quitey quite.

*

*

FREEDOM

LIBERTY *

and TINSEL   *

having one hard time looking for one good time,

you'll stop me because you've BEEN through this before

this right twisted HERE

this FREEDOM

this LIBERTY

and this TINSEL;

it wasn't curiosity killed that cat

it was a combination of THIS and . . . THAT, mostly

<u>THIS</u>:

onto that rainbow for one made dream,

Freedom is the right to choose WHICH ICE CREAM

that's right;

Liberty AND Tinsel,

Freedom is what your greaty-great grandfathers fought

for <u>YOU</u>

and liberty, your grandfathers for <u>YOU</u>

Tinsel is what you ACTUALLY GOT children;

more than you'll ever FUCK

Freedom is just a symbol

but then again;

SO AM I

from *Etymology of Screams*

I return there. Taken back, the force pulls its gravity, a rain of sequences brimming with opulence. Reversing into fortune. I am unfortunate, disproportionally forced down against my will, held up against the image of an aberration. I can't help it. It's not right. It's wrong but it always feels right.

The victim and his fantasy, sleeping in old spaces and murdering his cringes. The attack is forefrontal, behind is a melifluent agreement, but the attack is out front. It takes off my face. And with it, a last chance of redemption. 'Hold it, that's not right. I never meant that.' It's this: I ache above board. Radiant, burning. And when the kiss to my blisters unsalivates the balm, then, I will be lost to ruin. I live and revile.

A contemptible thing inside me, living alongside me, a wink to one side, deathly but urgent. I want to let go here. To leak with the wetness of life. Not death, death is just dry. I pushed. And then pushed back. I could kill before writing of death. I have to let it. To let: a request, proposal or command. Ask me what hurts and then watch me dissolve inside splinters. Sucked back in exactly where I want to escape.

I can't, can not. Where hope persists it is futile: you want to hope and then fake it, surge on. No need for anything more than the need itself. It's in here, a page bespeaking another page and then... pages of it trembling with forlorn derision. A happy ending. It all meets again joined up within me. Not eating me, I'm ate. A thread of scars feasting. At the central cornu and from there, bite into the fluid and chew. Masticate this breath. Walk out of here with this offal rubbed into me, yearning for birth in its dreaming text. Eating my words, returning, not singly, but more often collected.

4 Cacophonies

Classlocked, bawed
wi' wasparound
a geek culture, recidivist
visions
cranx incawporated non-
cute tangs, whump cartwheeling
I said that, said tell
palpably, its moment - 'ously' -
um mentum, nurturin'
menthol static, the
closedown
last hospice befaw
grrr - acious acts per spire
not t'clatter the
grutche one face into exotica
or to any thing less but faith

an easement dragged slyly down to own
"your praise for the rhyzome".
Writing in writing
goeth home daily
to teutonisms, to ethno-jazz
to romance
bait for rubalong futility symbols
a fear is klicking off, worrying
too earlye much
roundalong leaved and writhing

Manual act/ivity
pro-thesis, sh, shaving rituals
for markings at gunpoint:
'*so its daggers before dungeons because*
guns stunk of din . . . '

com'on com'on
- *wrunga dunga* -
ringin' up Gunga Din
sites spittling with powder
a tale-dragger
comes crawling out westways ~~before~~ and then
leastways, ways out
into casts of reliquary
connective spacings of
tongue, chewing for tethers,
feathers and woods in the offings

undergrowfs built for sissies, "the

grinding up glaciers,

plastics-held furrows": requisitioned,

compositioned to just trust

the replacement, old roots

destinationed/decimationed

as an uttermost

explosioned beyond chance landings

in gear.

Because that's enough

panegyric distinctions

bet. murder and suicide, death on screen, scam of fake.

Fake enough.

I went looking for some ROOTS
but everywhere was SHUT
went messaging but lost,
lost out to mess of
clickages

the lifetaker's   at the
composites for to settle   hearths
ears echolaolia for two functions schore
I and my/o/my
so-so creaks aroun' the squalid
fort   /   //
for only sound   / /
floods in ebbs/kickbacks

poor semiotics,

worse conversation, your

failure is to conversion

. . . pabapam pabapam pabapampa/clack:

'*cohercion's a jailor you met*

in your rearview next wednesday. . .'

like Item 1: a map of good coffee stains made good again

Item 4a: a swab of fluids, moodily

absorped in the fibre

of being cussed.

'*you dont need it*'

'- of course that sometimes helps'

You mean '*need nightly*' - '*to make a mends*' ?

'*but that's all well,*'

'*well that*' or '*whelps.*'

It's reading east again.

Real 'isms'
work up scratched my skull again
said to be good for you
but in this sole context of
English and . . .
ellipsis,
drama,
the urge to lose fingers, or lingus,
just one at each time,
repels the inaction:
nuthin's been done before
everything's bin dun
eg: 'language's muscular detonations in us. . .'
or the muscular detonations of lingo
'Ah. . . us!'
Denotations

much gaping and pausing
gaps 'capture', restrain a vox weight for
gestural sighting
dragging the whole length, the whole
mess of leg, second, round,
slowly, hand,
feels floor the walls
rightly, white tracks
unzipped, retraining
hunger-that-is-always-the-same.
The spaced territory,
the figure has
mention of mediance in the next
house along.
It says: Quite rightly, quite so.

from *Lives of the Saints*

Saint Agnes

Sovereignty or not between our page. A whistle broken up with wings, solder holds down a hemp belt that separates these alphas from delta, simply form and function founded. The U-front out of a weave of pallia. And on the arc of its ejection, is lost for curling into lines. The egress battened, fair fasten how it falls into spaces that are spared. Our readiness. Is bliss.

Saint Augustine

And certainly commensurably a roadsized eatery and convex past. In heraldry we wait. Brought in to cataloguing options, congesting them and offering seams of embarkation. As vandals. Conversion is effortless, maternalised in runs. Which qualities are quarantined inflexions, prandial in scope? The mange and gout of partially captured villanelles.

Saint Bartholomew

Proportionate to disguise in the ruse. Cro-magnify the slips of sought out variations. Cannibalise directions to mesopotamia. The stink. A rude miscreant within the drawl of measured pulp. 'I want tar'. Nectar and water. Where quicksand flays, continue with packaging the typeface. A twitch of skin. It won't be listening. Caradoc's seventh month of maritime fears exactly.

Saint Catherine of Siena

An amphitheatre staged persuasions in its ricket timbers. In intervals the talk is of its quantitude as time. The bee-line diademic strategies implode, sweat of added incumbents amongst the most impure of thinkers. Planetary influence figured out as welts, computed and written in. A plastic tube is waiting for its mount, an answer lives. In haste, life pictures an address along its side.

Saint Clare

Beside it never happened. Redoubt agreed terms. Aloud herd, O wence would it matter? On televisions the monstrous fist is ruralist. War nerves closed in, hold on to this yale. At the far end of dark indices begins sorrow's new place in a mosaic. Everything that fits is now bigger. Chattersome claws over twilight. Three pennies spilt for more thoughts. And mostly, there never is enough substance to fill out.

Saint Clement I of Rome

Consternation in phalanx tests germ resolve. Cost choirs meet daily and yearn for a sawn fleet. Bar rapids bickering reduced in the fight against ribaldry. An epidemic around anchors. Reflectors. My murmurs have pauses any time near to down time but racing continues just after the result. Why mention the moribund so soon after publicised resentment? Looks closer in respect.

Saint Dominic

Is dermis defeated in spotting out the ropes? Flick-stoppered, flash-handled wed through the brotherhood of fortitude. Traces of asphalt are only inspected halfway to overmaking orders. The pen piles the platitudes swilled back with pandemic. O slaughter, cry dominance. One down into old tally can cost-cut your custer. A dog in the midst of its murderous in-crust. Demented, huster call this one as out.

Saint Dympna

One gradient lasted, remorse spatting in. Noetic recounters, pollinium as phatic. Quincunx awaits us, to try to dismember those waves. Flattened ingredients. In only one moment of coral thought best kept on the high cornered shelf. This shivers all night perceiving the parts of a parchment disrobed. Oh help me, chime frost in your caucas. Amential in always reacting.

Saint Gall

The why is paused. Into the melatating acidity is poured a correctant. Angel dime willow cantata. Gerund beside gerund not cancelling. A loaded pressure, don't wait before time takes its place, does what? The form of a blackbird, ah Gloria. In fact infested. Grow up again and gratify grammatical oracular capacities. When one flight is called, move on mostly to fresh breeze. Four hundred years used to mean on piece in the hereafter. And rightly.

Saint Julian the Hospitaller

You need to lift up the sheets before wading in. Or maybe that's your call where your will takes you outside of your leash. With the bodily, at least, in place of stance*, (pretext always behind I.D.), the eyes are the last things you'll need. Insert me here, the universal re-tread. Penence at the last.

*Ideological.

Saint Catherine dei Ricci

Full bodied around the holy sprite, the agony and many shattering stories spill out nonetheless through her/him. Don't squander our swansong it listens to us from inside where night times elapse. But there's a day of thunder come round again and the hands are to meet in one clap. I'm sliding, which scene is it comes first?

Saint Valentine

With bracelets, a chance for lost childhood returns with the birds each year. Within, there's no sleep for me that doesn't come from you. Recycling the myths of invincibles yet again, there is, all the same, a call for our tenderness. I don't want to sing flop and fly. Discovered in flying, inflated with much more than our eyrie we too lose our heads.

meg bateman

Fhir luraich 's fhir àlainn

Fhir luraich 's fhir àlainn,
thug thu dàn gu mo bhilean,

Tobar uisge ghil chraobhaich
a' taomadh thar nan creagan,

Feur caoin agus raineach
a' glasadh mo shliosan;

Tha do leabaidh sa chanach,
gairm ghuilbneach air iteig.

Tha ceòban cùbhraidh na Màighe
a' teàrnadh mu mo thimcheall,

'S e a' toirt suilt agus gutha
dham fhuinn fada dìomhain,

Fhir luraich 's fhir àlainn,
thug thu dàn gu mo bhilean.

O bonnie man, lovely man

O bonnie man, lovely man,
you've brought a song to my lips,

A spring of clear gushing water
spilling over the rocks,

Soft grasses and bracken
covering my slopes with green;

Your bed is in cotton-grass
With curlews calling in flight,

Maytime's sweet drizzle
is settling about me,

Giving mirth and voice
to my soils long barren,

O bonnie man, lovely man,
you've brought a song to my lips.

Aotromachd

B' e d' aotromachd a rinn mo thàladh,
aotromachd do chainnte 's do ghàire,
aotromachd do lethchinn nam làmhan,
d' aotromachd lurach ùr mhàlda;
agus 's e aotromachd do phòige
a tha a' cur trasg air mo bheòil-sa,
is 's e aotromachd do ghlaic mum chuairt-sa
a leigeas seachad leis an t-sruth mi.

Lightness

It was your lightness that drew me,
the lightness of your talk and your laughter,
the lightness of your cheek in my hands,
your sweet gentle modest lightness;
and it is the lightness of your kiss
that is starving my mouth,
and the lightness of your embrace
that will let me go adrift.

Tha ceann casarlach mo leannain

Tha ceann casarlach mo leannain
mìn rim amhaich,
's mo chorragan nan ruith thar a lethchinn
's a' slìobadh a bhilean cadalach;

Ach is mìne fhathast mala
an fhir agus a ghaol air fuaradh,
nach cuimhnich a-nochd ar n-aighear
is gàirdeanan eile ga shuaineadh.

My lover's curly head

My lover's curly head
is soft against my neck,
as my fingers run down his cheek
and stroke his sleepy lips;

But softer yet the brow
of the one whose love has grown cold,
who tonight will not recall our joy
as he lies in other arms.

Dè 'm math dhòmhsa

Dè 'm math dhòmhsa
a bhith nam laighe fodhad,
thusa bu reul-iùil
m' uile thograidh,
's do chorp trom a-nist
gam bhrùthadh ris an talamh,
a' dubhadh às nan speuran
is lainnir reultan fad' às?

What good is it to me

What good is it to me
to be lying below you,
you who were the pole-star
that drew my longing,
with your heavy body now
crushing me to the ground,
blotting out the skies
and the lure of distant stars?

Gu luathghaireach aoibhinn laighinn leat

Gu luathghaireach aoibhinn laighinn leat, a luaidh,
do cheann tùrsach na eudail nam uchd,
mura b' adhbhar bròin mi paisgte nad làmhan –
dearbhadh cinnteach air smàladh do mhiann.

Oh gladly, gladly would I lie with you

Oh gladly, gladly would I lie with you, my darling,
your sad head a treasure in my breast,
if, held in your arms, I were not part of your grief –
certain proof of the smooring of your dreams.

'S toigh leam an taigh seo

'S toigh leam an taigh seo
a ruigeas mi tro mhuir de chuinneig-mhighe,
an càr air a bhualadh
le meapaidean buidhe fliuch de chonasg.

An leanabh na chadal,
siùbhlaidh mi na rumannan,
casan loma air clàran loma,
's mi a' sireadh nan taibhsean
a dh'fhàg an dìleab seo de chiùineas,
aig an nochd an anail san fheur fhada
na flùraichean purpaidh is gorma.

A dh'oidhche laighidh mi nam chaithris
fo thorann an uisge air na sglèatan,
fo thorann boile mo thoileachais
nach fhaic duine,
is sa mhadainn mus dùisg an leanabh
èisdidh mi ri stairirich nan gobhlan-gaoithe
is iad trang mun àl fon mhullach.

Eiridh leòmainn bheaga gheala
mu ar casan san drùchd;
gus an till sinn cha chluinn duine
an guilbneach os cionn nam pàircean,

I love this house

I love this house
that I reach through a sea of lady's lace,
the car buffeted
by wet yellow mops of broom.

With the child asleep,
I wander from room to room,
bare feet on bare floorboards,
seeking the ghosts
who left this legacy of calm,
whose breath appears in the long grass
as blue and purple flowers.

At night I lie awake
under the thundering rain on the slates,
under the thundering outrage of my happiness
that no-one sees,
and in the morning before the child wakens
I listen to the scuffling of the martins,
attending to their brood below the eaves.

Little white moths flutter
round our legs in the dew;
till we come home no-one will hear
the curlew above the fields, its call

a ghàir a' gluganaich mar fhìon à botal;
chan fhaic duine
na coineanaich mun fhaiche,
is an taigh na sheasamh aig ceann an rathaid,
a chùl ris an iodhlainn far an tionndaidh am posta
's a bheul ris a' ghàrradh fa chomhair na beinne.

Ged a sguabadh bhuam na-huile

Ged a sguabadh bhuam na-huile
a bhuilich an gràdh na lànachd,
chan olc leam dinneadh an reothairt
no pian is tosd a thràghaidh,

Oir sheòl mi sàl air òradh
ne chlàr lòghmhor neo-chrìochnach
is nuair a dh'fheuch mi a thomhas
fhuair mi sonas gun ìochdar,

'S mi ruith ron ghaoith mhiannaich,
m' eathar fo iarmailt reultaich
an tòir air gach sòlas san t-saoghal
gus a thaomadh an uchd m' eudail.

like wine gurgling from a bottle;
no-one will see
the rabbits round the lawn
of the house that stands at the end of the track,
its back to the yard where the postman turns
and its front to the garden, looking onto the hill.

Though everything has been swept away

Though everything has been swept away
that love granted at its fulness,
I do not regret the onrush of the tide
or the pain and silence of its ebbing,

For I've sailed a sea turned gold,
a gleaming plain without limit,
and when I tried to gauge its depth
I found no bottom to my bliss,

Running before the darling wind,
my boat under a star-filled sky,
in search of every delight in the world
to pour out in my treasure's lap.

Mathair

Bha sinn a' coimhead nan rionnag
mus do thionndaidh sinn a-steach leis na coin
is thuirt thu gum bu mhithich dhut
na h-ainmean aca ionnsachadh gu ceart.

Ach chan fhada gus am bi thu fhèin nam measg
's is mis' a bhios a' feuchainn ri d' ainmeachadh,
thusa aig nach fhaca mi do nàdar
ach mar priobadh an cuid solais –

Is tu riamh an ceann do dhleasdanais,
mu chòcaireachd, chaoraich, leabhraichean;
eil fhios an d'fhuair thu do dhìol
airson do dheataim is spàirn is sgìths?

O gun lasainn de dh'aighear annad
a leigeadh leam d' fhaicinn gu slàn
no chan fhaide thu bhuam nuair a shiùbhlas tu
na bha thu rim thaobh a-nochd.

Mother

We looked at the stars for a while
before we turned in with the dogs,
and you said it was high time
you learned their names properly.

But soon you will be amongst them yourself
and I will be the one trying to name you;
you whose nature I have seen
only as their faint points of light –

As you labour behind duty,
behind pots and pans, sheep, books;
who knows if you have your reward
for your care and effort and exhaustion?

I wish I could kindle a joy in you
that would let me see you whole
or you won't be further from me when you go
than you were tonight by my side.

Caraid Sgoile

Tha an rùm dìreach mar a bha e
na feasgairean ud a chuir sinn seachad
nar laighe air ar blian ron teine,
a sholas a' mire air a' phiano,
air na dealbhan de sheanairean is shinn-seanairean,
na cùirtearan tiugha a' dùnadh às na h-oidhche.
Tha a' mhàthair a' gabhail mo naidheachd,
is cuimhne aice air gach duine againn,
tha am bodach fhathast a' gearan
mar a chaidh na Tòraidhean bhuaithe,
ach mo charaid-sgoile,
chan aithnichinn i,
's i gu giùigeach, trom,
a' dèanamh strì ri gàire far an iomchaidh. . .
is thig stad nam sheanchas
mu cholaisdean, dhreuchdan, phòsaidhean, naoidheanan. . .
"Agus dè tha dol agaibhse?"
 (Feumar a' cheist a chur orra.)
"A' dèanamh ar dìcheall. . .
An druim a' cur dragh air Dad. . ."
Dìreach mus nach bi càil ri chur an cèill ach bròn,
dìreach mus nach bi càil ri rùsgadh ach call,
èiridh mi.

School Friend

The room is just as it was
those evenings we spent
lying on our tummies at the fire,
the flamelight flickering on the piano,
on the paintings of grandfathers and great-grandfathers,
the thick curtains keeping out the night.
The mother asks for my news,
remembering everyone by name,
the old man is still complaining
how the Tories went downhill,
but my school friend –
I wouldn't have known her,
round-shouldered, heavy,
striving to laugh at the right places. . .
and my account falters
of colleges, careers, marriages, babies. . .
"And how are all of you?"
 (The question has to be asked.)
"Doing our best. . .
 Poor Dad's being bothered by his back. . ."
 Just before there is nothing to speak of but sorrow,
 just before there is nothing to show but loss,
 I stand up.

Tuitidh ar faileasan às a' chonservatory,
tarsainn air an rèidhlean
far an cluicheamaid is dreasaichean geala oirnn.
Thèid mi seachad air a' chraoibh
anns am faca sinn uair tro na geugan
ùbhlan òr-bhuidhe
a' deàrrsadh fo chomhair na guirme. . .
Aig a' gheata tionndaidhidh mi
is tha làmh mo charaid air a leth-thogail
ann an comharra nach eil i cinnteach às.
Togaidh mise mo làmh-sa – slàn
le ar n-òige, le aotromachd, gealladh. . .
Bhriseadh an cridhe
mur b' e deàrrsadh an cuid coibhneis.

Our shadows slant out of the conservatory,
across the lawn
where we used to flit in white frocks.
I pass under the tree
where once we saw through the shady branches
golden apples
shining against the endless blue. . .
And at the gate I turn
and my friend's hand is half-raised
in a gesture she is not sure of.
I raise my hand – farewell
to childhood, to joy, to promise. . .
The heart would break
if it wasn't for the gleam of their kindness.

An Glaschu

Abair sealbh is sonas
bhith tachairt air an t-sràid riut,
a' ghrian a' deàrrsadh,
na bàraichean fosgailt'…

Och, abair nàire
bhith gun smuain ri cur an cèill,
m' inntinn glacte gu lèir
led àilleachd.

In Glasgow

What bliss and good fortune
to meet you in the street,
the sun shining
the bars open…

What mortification
to think of nothing to say,
my mind transfixed
by how lovely you're looking.

A chionn 's gu robh mi measail air

Thigeadh e thugam
nuair a bha e air mhisg
  a chionn 's gu robh mi measail air.

Dhèanainn tì dha
is dh'èisdinn ris
  a chionn 's gu robh mi measail air.

Sguir e den òl
is rinn mi gàirdeachas leis
  a chionn 's gu robh mi measail air.

Nist, cha tig e tuilleadh
is nì e tàir orm
  a chionn 's gu robh mi measail air.

Because I was so fond of him

He used to come to me
when he was drunk
  because I was so fond of him.

I'd make him tea
and listen to him
  because I was so fond of him.

He stopped the drink
and I was pleased for him
  because I was so fond of him.

Now he comes no more,
indeed he despises me,
  because I was so fond of him.

khaled hakim

Letter to Antin

Dear Mr Antin

This is part of the poem. I wonder if yd be interested in some of my performativ werk. Ive lately been occupyd w/ episolary forms, wich is an enactment of riting. I realy wanted to giv a long piece, my 2nd Letter to Brakhage. This is a performans poem wch givs y/ an idea of wat i do in performans & episolary.

I wen to the Poetry Library insid the Festival hal. A realy swanky place. & i was dying to go to the toilet first wich is conveniently just outside it on the 5th Level. & inside wer a cuple of ruff trayd who sort of flattend themselvs up against th urinals syde by syde & lookt at me out the corner of thr eye.

& id only gon in to wash up. I thght, Oh its a tee room – I thght it was odd this place in the Festival Hall outsid the Poetry Libry shd be chose to coksuck, & what kynd of clientel they got. & i lyked that. It felt lyk poetry was beeng kept alive. Caus ther wer mor peple in the toilet than th libry.

Its the best stockt plais for new poetry & peeriodicals anywher heer, & id gon in to check up on a poet w/ affinitees – David Antin, & i notisd how morglike it was – somwon was asleep & otherwys it was in profownd

Ive com to be unable realy to rede w/o mowthing. I remember i was trying to rede Rimbaud & lern French, & im speking it to get the hang. After 3 weeks i wen into the Central Libry & took down a book, & i fownd cauz i cdnt actually *say* the words w/o disturbing other peple &

them thinking i was thick – i literaly cdnt understand it. Saying translyted the sines. If i tryd doing it sowndles – as weve al lernt – i cdnt reed.

I waz thinking this caus id just been reding Onians abowt the Gk Homeric lokation of the seet of consciusnes or inteligens (phrenes) in the lungs – lyk children think, thauwt is in the mouth.

They cald me *Owwa* in Bangladesh, becaus i wasnt fluent in Bengali, & not beeng fluent in langwage i had no idiom of ordnary lif. It meens idiot, literaly dumm. They wernt teken in by my books.

This is how peeple red. I was in that Poetry library w/ all its roling stacks wich is ment as absolute repozitory or depozitry, & intrested peopl – profeshnals – com & reserch. I dont kno what for. Its hard me for not to wish i was w/ the tee room boyz in the toylet. I thawt i shd hav gon in & sd *Lissen if yu dont giv me som of yor ars im gonna stick my fist up it.* Im caerful of my fascist impuls to burn appropriat librys.

I recal reding abowt St Ambrose hoo was a wunder to the other monks becauz he cd actualy rede w/p mooving his lips. Do ye kno what the cells thees carrels wer for – it was so they dint disturb other monks wen reding the Bible. Becus nowon was abl to reed silently. Becaus we hav learnt to *see* nothing. Dont worry if i tawk beneth you – its part of the grater redundancie of orality – y/ can drop in or owt, becuse i dont speke to a supereleet – of one.

I didnt hav to think of this as a poem. The occazion of poetrie is simply a decision. I gus in th toilet theyr disturbd felating. I gos into th libry its unnatural qwiet, becaus thouht is in th mouth. Its not becuz Antin was saying somthing abowt myth muthos is simply saying

45

Rather the poetic brain begins organizing th flux of my living into connexion. I think in form.

Im looking up a talk poet whos work isnt even a scor, only a record; its only strange it dosnt mak sens mor ofen. Im lookin up a magazene Talus i can giv somthing to, & now ive had the idea i can transpoze this into a Letter to Antin.

Dere Mr Antin, yr poem tawkd me out of my afair. Wed bin having a ruff time anyway & im down ere cauz of it. This publick occazion poem that seems to be looking for principls of agreement in lov, in mariage, & wch pretends to a matur judgemnt, & wch is reely looking for a way out yr prezent afair. Ye can see it in this pat opposition, analogie w/ the story abowt yr erlier affaer wch is so obviusly unsatisfactory, & Eli hoo is so obviusly somthing els – oh *yeeah*. I dont kno if yu kno it. I usd th poem (found) as a sign, as magik.

Im so misrable Mr Antin – I just watcht the Watson-Eubank fiht & when he yad him down i jumpt up & bangd my hed against the beem i hadnt been so happy all week; & wen the referee stopt the fiyt i hadnt been so unhappy al week. Three seconds later Eubank got up & knokd down Watson. It meks me think thoz Budhist w/ thr distrust of emotion, this paranoyac retreet from activitie into the mandarin contemplativ, maybe they got it rite. If Abbie ad been ther id hav puncht the shit ourof her. In my poems im always the most ridickulus won.

I did a performance last tym wich dint werk becuz i got cawt up w/ yr Sokratic curv of inqwirie insted of keeping to my short agressiv – in, owt. I dont want nufin to do w/ al that sweet reesonablnes saintly seeking after process

Look at this performanse poem – its al bleeding level discours like wat yu do – whers the gimicks the acting i stick in look at thes fuckin paragrafs, im suckt into tropes that arent nemonic

the more i kno abowt yr work the less i wanna no – i shd stick w/ the fiers campiness. Hoo can bor peeple better w/ yr mode

same w/ that L=A=N=G=W=I=G=E textualitie guff they starrid afecting me owt of wat i doo – what *do* i do – a lone popular polemick against the cors of poetick *use* & transmishon sins the Renaisance. Im caerful of my conformist streek.

Wen ise a kid & had suss but i always fownd it dificult to argu my intuicions from werking clas values – becauz langwage & reazon wer the langwij & reson of a class literat; & i had to lern the langwige of categories to lern i didn hav the langwage of categoris

I realiz im being drawn into dogmatizing oral modes, cauz nobody nos wat im doing, so not only do i hate all practicioners of anything that looks lyk vers, i ate everythink that dosnt qwestion why its in a book, the whol fuking inteeriorizd seeking after identity wch is the excuse for poeticks

hyding in som fen for 12 yers then inflicting craftid pietis on us – drop ded git.

I jus thowht Mr Antin yd lyk to kno that yre not qwite an isolated voyce, if not a sad lonelie old man w/out my lov then furrowing a lon trayl up yr arsole. Thers somwon in Birmingam hoo was doing poems w/ a prozody of comutativ verbiag, caus wat the fuck, & I know hoo yu ar, & heer wer at the interfase of a hole changeover from an irelevant cultur – but nobodie nows it

Birmingham Nov 91

Letter for S

Dar S_____

my Tomswood, damson sqwash pavements my girdeld limits, yor seecret tarmac paths deluge bramble, my cockt hat plantasion filld with boare, the barb roling nets red & blackbrie – a finger gos down & plucks th hares & bursting pods apart

my beares, lov tawht to eet th berries dirt

th plum delectabel distanse, th various tangle & stinging buttonhole, & yor Brasher boots & a skirt for curious insect, the sole scrunching unnown orderz

a little finger feel a firey apples bum, my lov tauht me bite the green pimple, pressing th many grassis owr shirtskin

we lookd down at the cables & fantastick insect ticks & mites to share owr skin my lov, but I look for hymenoptera th fairy flyz, the insect lover givz up to biytes

so much berry world, colour clots to whomy lov – she arguing for God & me arguing for the grasses, withowt baer or deer, my wood hartbraking harvest

liht lowers & brings up hether wash, a faery tree, & springing jeep ruts; paiynters painted liyhte in infinit derivacion, & saw more stars & pantographs to plot th growth of enclozure

evrywaere attendant brissle & sensilla scratch

but genre retired, & I never stood with an eazel looking at nature like a prick

whaere do we go for low sensuousnes & delayd gratification my lov;

modernity screening owt projecsion sympathie narrativ, sufferd me to underrite middleclass valuz

gave up conceptual prozodiz the good opinion of my peers, how mimesis & temporizing plague the maker, & internet porn, for yoo my lov

& craep leeves prinkt rust

I am leeding yoo a baerly ther path, wich coms of my corupsion, & asking pathetick qwestions, I want yu thair

buxom ruff roling to the edges dark thickit, fructus & yor old wood, yor dwindling integument & my late com

stripping diseasd skin, dig for bloody flowerd wolvz,

renewing landscape peepld lack, th waterfawling tree, th rattling green, liyht is flowing thru & tyme is froing thru…

Hey lov, I cannot marry you for there is no use, I was a postmodern cliche & cudnt liv th grate metanarrativ of free libraris until I cam up against the metanarative of multiculturalizm

a demographick of aestheets becom sqwatters, or eqwally chic drug uzers, but modern poetri chose them for its sexless colorles brood, & I believd them wen they didnt say class was relevent

we joind you to have no money, no institucional capital, & virtuous effacement; mothers aquird Welfar system competens & broht us up alon, & I a partial subject have no meens to join the human race.

Yoo think if only I deliver you fundamental meening weel eaze up & liv ever after –

I was talking to some peple & they wer goin on lyk – Well I havnt red the er, but Im sure thers a differens bitween David Koraish & other loony charismaticks lik Jesus, becus hee was acting out of lov, & I sed Wel therz a doctrin selflesly painted for many centurys, but we ar now sceptickal abowt the comission of baby Jeesus to th nekked nativs

Its mor interesting than God. Also God isnt simple enouf. It is. It is not. It is

But I'm in love with you – hey yoo!

gerrin drawn back to th limit for molten skyz molten God that poets tymelesly doo,

my autonomous realm, contaminated by neither kulture nor theery nor any fuckin houzing estates

how scool of Lorrain haz diffrent religius liyht to indiffrent Moneys – how my representacion of Lascauw as a lantern show is better than yor exhibicion

but yoo can mak a diffrens. Yoo can decide this barbarick incizion is beter than that barbarick infibulasion,

Thoz discriminasions, Miles, oh finicking surfaciz, warrisit they do! Som politicks morr than langwage! I can sit at a table w/ five poets & cunnilinguas all rownd & noone can tell – sure that poetrie matters, oh I wish I cud, oh I wish I cud

descry thoz nonreturners riting water, whoz words disolve as soon as red & reform when yoo reed again

& fell into noself to do the feeling, reducd to relacsionships of overlaping, th paynted surfase becom the ethical plane

geting owt of my maids bed after the trifling Pimpernel crying Oh, Master Champion make me a good girl agen!

& chose immemorial logos,

but heere coms the invazion of cricket on PCP with vengeful Gods & normativ sexual relacions

lemme remember the sense…

Dear Andrew, yoo ever been at a conference where a sociology of poetries is denied yr own marginal poetics – because bad ptry only can be analysed but yr practice needs only the appreciation of the good…Oh yeah, you have –

I got on the British Poetries site yesterday for the first time, to have sprayed my sign in the pecking orders

the etiolation, the dues – why didnt I stick to wanking –

Andrew, I cant do it, I'm going bonkers w/ incredulity of the metanarrative of justice, & the world introjecting me up the ass. & those small discriminacions –

am I a poet – or a poet. You remember th reding yu didnt go to, & I wantid to do somthing with this. Some new register – in a space

I'd been thinking about – I was in my Oxfam shop – reprodusing th tape of Idi Amin intervewing hiz Bishop teling his soldjers – Kickk him! Kickk him! Mek him crawwrl!

This goverment oficial gets visited & the officer swings his 3 yer old kid by th feet & smashes his brains on th wall, & then the tribal chief who upset a neiybour rival who got the paras in – I hav a vaig pictur its by a river or the vilage pool they make him kill hiz six wives & hiz children then hack his arms off on a ston & let him crawl to som hospital to dictate this story.

But the saddest fuck this lil Paki shopkeeper pickd up by the police siting in his cell racking hiz brain what heez don, wile sound of bloks screeming lik animals, & then boots com & th keys clank, & in coms the biggest mother gorrila. Shopkeeper doznt kno wat to say but th gard stamps over withowt a word he kicks the most teeth & shit out. Wile hiz lying ther, he gets this bucket of piss & shit over him, & hees left with the fliyz & stink & blod. In the niht, he heers th dor go, & this guard carrying a carbord box, he thinks it miht be food. But its chuckt in & th box just explodz with theze crazd starving rats all thru the niyht my litle Paki fiyting off ther attacks.

It was in my head, so disruptiv, riyht to the edge of presense agen, but it looks so dull & perfunctory. Were missing the authenticitie of the affidavit, an exhabicionist record the experiens poem in th shop – but I *promiss* therz a way to make it Hans Haacke

to be poetri & not poetre at th same tiyme

I waz a teenage teenager, with authentick noselvs, but I red it – morr aphid cookd in a sunfleck!

I waz a citie boy, filling hills with Welsh gorillas dying from flu, & dirigible folly

bur I red it purple loosestrife & docks, so wele find it strange jumping phasmida –

I am leeding you therr, & asking pathetick qwestions – Wat was it like to liv at the end of th centurie az a subject of poetrie – yoo viviparus wastrels…

but I'm in love with you – I'm in love with yoo – hey yoou!

London July 99

Run Pm

After i mist the morning, this shud hav been a Hymn to Liyht.

Seeing with Liyt is rare, & springliyt is rarest. The noze flummoxt w/ smel.

So otherwiz it is slugish, go for a run. Owt from a Cup final. & later the Bregenzer festspiel & later

Economick in stryd. Runing w/ incorruptibl joynts, tender, w/ keez & a sayfty pin holding my flys.

& on Church Hil not for th first tym the evry erth in relaciun blu to wite sky, unseen crowding up city.

hevy underfoot park & trot.

Heer acros th fencing, the ruind wiyt ston of th semetary. O yeah, obvius the Muzlim graivs wer busted at th base, just the imigrant slabs, paranoack heresay. But it al looks nackerd hill.

Trot, war fame sun has not dryd the edges.

Waer is the runing poem going revisited, why is the pm. Ar we pretending to see my lov

Ya, Kev. But we must run, for Imelda is again too much, & i too litel... I dont wannu do it anymor. Its broke down

this diction of ezy clipt, thats the form of day to day epifenomenalism – history all is history

I dont understand wy uze thees special modes, watever historical speech patern – the excizion of articls, prepozicion, an overburdening copula – or the overburdening indeterminat prepozicions stragling th liyn –

nowon qwestions why this, wy poetry. Wy this exacted flux

It doznt mayk sens to me, non of it ansers. Why this –

lapidary of sens.

Tayk th cirkit, & at the park bowndary, go bak

Heer broken acsess to Handsworth semetry, shd be gud for som thowhts. But no notebook so no poem.

& straitway ther snapt crossiz & the fawlen stonz: ah lying in th shalow bed, a carven three foot figur, marbel w/ its hed mising – othersiz shd i hav nickt it. Did somwon realy chizel clasical folds liyk thoze reproducsions.

Wawk down the wooded sunlit pyls: but no notbook so no poem. But afeckting inscriptions of Edwardian; & familis under toomstone, but no glases. & leningtoos & vandalizd.

Just wun – perhaps a suspicius congregacion over at Church Hill – a blak broken tablet, grayt falen sheald, & at its shard end held water in basin. & at its hed inscripcion had pited & honeycomd owt in atricion, & also holows, as armadillo osify into holows.

But ther waz only a baer inoquous tree to look up. & heer won fantastick trunk limb that grew over into a whiplash.

So thru, looking for the muslims his unkle, spiting skin went thru & thru th genrel mischif who sez deth is the end of truble.

Run poem revizit the original isnt –

I dont understand wat this dictiun is – to run thru 6 monkeys tapping typriters hoo wil eventualy discover the syntactik relaycions to poetry is, cuz i dont kno

if styl *parataxis* is expreshion of forms of fals conshiusnes, then synapsiz colapst, veleity working thru syntax

Wy this – wy this

This is th part from the other siyd of th fens. The magpys, as i wawkt rownd, & up, & bak to th top. Valted the mucus wal, onto th rode. Lets run. Lets run bak onions. So trot hyding my flyz.

Th lihte is stil so hony it hurts.

O shit! heer this joyus girl, i duckt, on Heethfeild Rd is thumming a lift

That hurts me so. This is th sanctiun to rite this – but not yoo to reed. Ile never stop riting proze.

oh shit oh shit heer is the Breygenzer festspeil: hav i fukt won of the litel stage animals.

& then into Amazon raynforest with hiz dinner. & now a 30 yr old myopick asshole martinet acros Austrailia – having livd his lif bakward – how find his way bak into th nature destinie.

.... ooOoo ....

Pound me a Tarantela w/ Jewzharp

– Fuk off –
Its th Pitie we cant tayk!
Its th Pitee we cant tayk!

adrian clarke

from *Spectral Investments*

echoing subject equal to
the real marked down
in these words back
in the picture from
a neutral point keys
depress the record *decor*
his intention is transparent
doubled in the text
its object reeled off
in the leaden wash
dark wood of bookshelves
dead to the world
beyond the window last
prints of a will
the narrative counters frame
by frame the worm
at the centre spins
silk dresses <u>her</u> appearance
another dimension any resemblance
to persons discounted hard
to tell whose desire
freezes on the screen
say what you like
ADRIFT IN THE COSMOS
the culture bottomed out
demotic predicates fog an
option covered by the

theme business as usual
where x̲ cannot be
without y̲ units combine
the legend **EXIT** streets
illuminated with festive lights
their excess in perspective
an obscure rescue necessity
in the order gets
us nowhere scenarios fashion
2 holes cut price
women hurry past alien
and critical seems exact
shifting focus an awkward
ensemble aligns the image
things <u>are</u> the child
in the driving seat
want a cake "we"
fixed it WIPERS stet
unregenerate indexed *extra* inscribes
demand haecceity ecstatic produced
in the struggle to
be expected other elements
separate out 2 burning
halves unknot the belt
deferments harden the tip
visible confused it is
in the dominant system
the gag of flesh
that stroke in the
middle marked the least

again thickly forced out
the words the power
to make spells divorce
statistics felt her womb
with a guiltless climax
to stop her lips
he inserts a page

THIS COULD BE IT

a shadowless
moment receding
at the edge of
its aesthetic I
dares
the culture
dreamed of
on one plane only
with a ghostly
ambition
characters form
the issue
they're not
occulted by
pictures a code
repeats
fleshed in the
interval
when love has
gone

sense insists switch to
BiC prick the epidermis
scripting *DAD* reprints iterate
the system is closed
an official told reporters
police opened fire to
make sense of their
text an arrow of
retribution dictated to the
Prophet in airports and
suburbs paternal translates travelling
to the heart of
needles the people asked
to explain the Book
a rather arrogant fiction
with a certain global
objectivity after Friday prayers
in several parts of
the city midnight's children
whistle in the dark
as chandeliers extinguish laughter
frayed nerves with a
constant trajectory spread out
below temples lie drawn
on both banks *put*
up or shut up
this map is ground

displaced by the depiction
she wanders lewdly shopping
the skyline's hard brilliant
edge Boundary Road to
Queen Square a speculative
art pausing for breath
feeble bodied if exotically
RICH to a solitary
red numbering her possessions
"A nous deux maintenant"
as if truth were
on the other side
of this equation corporeity
sang with the pain
inherent in the drift
of signals context testifies
effaced a mysterious region
the ring passed through
deviance resolves a blade
glanced into snakes leaves
vaseline the flesh wresting
particulars bled from the
verge of a ghastly
blur *DEATH BEFORE DISHONOUR*
stopped her breath recursive
in the dingy light
of a formulation accounts

for itself a passage
reflecting oddities of the
rainbow beyond the door
spring restated as seductive
space to abolish this
obsession with a useless
return whose site rendered
coltsfoot bluebells from the
adjacent canal flowering in
its words specificity shapes
the real purpose hidden
in clover producers strip
show me and I'll
show you a paradigm
says nothing hired out
to its captive audience
a window gets smashed
by the piece with
a gloved hand choosing
which movie the dialect
frames "extrinsically" <u>moral</u> Black
Russian voices err through
static bands back from
the brink high heels
to sidewalk names limit
a literal silence a
speaker at a time

everything narrates desire adulterate
declared *in flagrante* bursts
into the residual image
with an abuse of
the metaphoric any old
totem couched in terms
of an admonition to

THE DEVIL IN DISGUISE

time to wake up
to a naive
resemblance
put on the successive
antidotes to
remembrance could
be on hooks could
be grommets rain
falls
before the £
plummets
the sun rises also
precisely when it
appears
the flag looks great
plagiarised rather
the stars

to the naked eye
what matter to relate
effect for symptom Washington
descends the steps in
pursuit of the title
with Monroe's face precedence
instamaticked the ideal constellation
a.k.a. a
community of writers fingered
by their appliances switched
to a double in
is out or *vice*
versa omitting a stage
on the other coast
where a shared grammar
brings home the goods
the transient observes El
= L = letters
collected he reads from
the text a pun
attended to hypostasize FACT
history resolves to tell
it all in variable
proportions as the colours
fade from the field
of contention this property
is dressed to kill
spillage from the psychedelic

lapse in a drizzle
of blossom commensurate with
a straitened prose followed
retrospectively to erase himself
in the gap an
epistemology brackets masked with
black hair mid Atlantic
throws little light on
an upturned biceps petals
scale to *AMERICAN WOMAN*
exotic in reverse from
the Victorian mirror's aquarian
depths traced in bold
the hearse serves to
recycle Marilyn's tenor spectrality
transcends "the classic vehicle"
THE MAIL 1st May
"a three foot cube"
sold for blades scraping
to extend the design
in 10 more years
right arms won't do
if familiar contraltos are
to raise the song

PEOPLE WITH LIKE MINDS

not impoverished simply
less
equal than the female
of the species in
the English language given
the world one tends
to defend yourself to
hold the ship on
course the tigress attacked
what Latin was 8
000 miles away in
the mists of time

it remains to wait
message obliterated in a
futile exchange Sunday **STRATFORD**
PLATFORM 3 depots containerpark
to the towerblock back
drop *hors commerce* through
an empty terrain lines
curve to the right
angle dip at the
intersection in the absence
of causes a random
bullet smashes a concept
to a scatter of
dots the screen dead
handed revisiting dizziness by
passed by the connections

nicholas johnson

Gillows Mohr

Are you goan an op Anley Burslem?
'n' op Anley firststop yis
Jis tek me t 5 towns caff n   for
drap me off ahr rownda bout bettyshop
my hunch is big I'm goan roun headcups
below skysheath I need polystyrene cup
yah lucazade amyl poppers chest expand ahn I've not
any monie dow but I'm still tanking on my homewins first over the Bonus
I doan call on Shilling the Singer at Festy Park
he's mebbe Penkull
where he sings or others swann
where he sings or others do

I tak a bike
get most tipoffs that way   it's easy bets happy mondays
I'm going round headcups dance to finley quayle, happy mondays i couldn't
bet yah kitkat's got silverfoil initstill
i can tell by snitch in paper
that way over bridge fur to Bengal Nitrate
no tooth's impeccable n yah shd see my forearms go
in a best's boy I bite at flies around my head Yis
n doan pour sucar in my coffee na more
Town. Play Station ADVANCERS I do not like green lights and ham
purple lights and tomato

yellow lights and meatpie Grey lights much Roger
n we go
uphill from Canal and rounded underpass
precision is one in the eye for me to Cheam or lower Station Road
round back precious
if canna bring Wigan forty-fives
next Tuesday not next Thursday Jains
then james brown mikey dread ONE LOVE
tubular pipes roun Shelton back
at night cold blasts vat factories
behind silver tracers vast the Infras
oh man   This is where bring war to
I know   sed it's sad   This' where bring bodies to
n count the haves & have nots
                              On pavement
i'm crossing roads while
my bike's ont pavement
while you're crossing roads your bike's going Shelton
Mowcop Longton it's business at depot
as Bikers or up all night but no awake
at Essential place
yuh need Zest or zinc or Lucaz
Aid
that's no head around my waist
diet pep C n I caint brek my head over That
I stand here allus hands around my beer
Sidewards I

skank to Viccy Hall but no one's ever there play good cept PIXIES
n that way in foyer - you dint see him, Shilling boy
Stop on Devious Corner   One Love
No truckstop
to Roaches hill with abbatoir candles awlupit
Round the V
from there you call on clouds as I do I need all the breath I got
who needs all breaths you got you're Inter Galactic
off him her both more kitkat   iss meks naw diffrence
foil glinting on the roaches
next week I'll go filmtheatre sit at the back watch *Clerks* again
I seen it ha'nt I?
I wont press flowers in your buke even if I live outside

dray me Rudyard reservoir in summer,
tho flowers yes an get time to pick em get time to pick em
doan give you nothing but odds
it is well and just
goes like that.
                    To the drains Singer. Get time to pick 'em

The Heron

Parabola: contemplating in all electrical phenomena the operation of a Law which reigns through all Nature, viz. the law of polarity, or the manifestation of one power by opposite forces.

I can't tell you all the names; I'm worried
about the birds rabbling the sky

Douglas Oliver

A pale yellow moon on the horizon
sluicing through rushes of vision,
evening raises and no human reconciles the hush
with what is ordained to ascend

the hush that is hurt from tumult of the agony
the wrenching of hearts from their shoals
silhouetted Hell among the Pleiades :
what makes you revile her for a decision you could not make?

A trade of every tumult,
despite every posit and rationale
a veering trade of abject weakness
in the silver straw

And what was the decision that you made
when you would mount an image
spotted on bronze photographs to my face,
a gaze you captured, against a stone wall had vanished?

If it is speech that installs probability
and events that cause and crescend are upon us
and no notation's found
then is it not enough to subvert the image
iridescent of a moon radiant on the blossoms
that fell   when a shoreline changed   and insisted on a
heartless sickening time, time without polarity or edifice?

A pale yellow moon on the shoreline,
soil properties thread to eerie glitter direct
our footsteps, and words jut from horseblood earth,
the moon goes abroad sluicing fields
coating gorse with a pristine fluid.

> The cold tumult
> of winter is on your sleeves
> you have decided on a whim
> to go outside the parabola,

> I walk abroad with my conscience,
> yet I have nothing to tell you,

I have admitted nothing
because I must hurt you with scorn.

It was not the cold beat of your eyes that led me
to the Pleiades field to see a heron alight and sever her prey,
the gainless guile of the creature that could not hover;
I detailed nothing of the meetings I hid from you;
it was not the pasts we shared led me away from you
but the savage turn of your head, from all that is unreconciled

Lovers in a pleat of cockiness, we have exchanged our gifts,
and I caught the hush of limbs against mine
breath and laughter round lips meant for another man

I caught the sound of a conduit in abject sobriety :
a silhouette of a heron rears up between
our bodies when we are naked and unsated,
our sinews are taut when her hands are roving,

if I lie beside you it is not because I have asked you
to lie beside you, but because I cannot resist you

I saw the vision of a man at a public ordeal
with a rope thread round his neck
that would slowly loosen
cast from an upstairs landing

I saw a man weep because he was a traitor
and a child walking abroad in the hills
ablaze with phosphor; my bonny rosehip lipped lad
my heart was in the highlands, above where the Aberdeen waters flow.

Savage turns of the head
levelling out a lunar scythe
you breathe in the phosphor breathe in the lime
at a rapid shoreline

Every word you uttered made me suffer,
every silence I obeyed :
what was the use of all that gesture
and pain, I did not see the Reason in that.

I was not alone in telling you
that the word had spent itself,
the sound of your anguish
burns in my head

It was not the shame I shared that led me away from you
but a conviction that my dialogue was not solely with you;
and because 'I talk only of voices either real or virtual in my ear'
I went down to where the heron fed on cold air streams
and because it was dark, 'across a sepia estuary where I felt freedom'

I could not see the heron supine on the shoreline
until I crouched down and Sirius was up;
not from its silhouette nor from reason could I find
a decision more painful to select

The ground lamp was turned to your face :
I saw you cry out and I knew your obvious rancour,
and if the coursing of blood
thru your blue veins could not be listened to
then I had no right to emote my anger,
we listened to the river, turbulent as our hearts
                              where Aberdeen waters flow.

My heart was in the highlands
and my eyes were on the shore line
I could not determine the Reason
there was only the silhouette of branches at low tilt

freathed with spume from a river's gradience :
how could I admit to my heart

that I was wrong in denying a Passion
for a person I spoke wrongly to

that I was wrong in lodging a discord
to the person I had come to distress

that I was wrong in bringing a discord
to a woman I had denied truth to?

from *Haul Song*

Snow thick on chapple
yard;   bright   stones
blink   refract
light not objects

The kitchen cloth night. See it!   Cervix high,
rethroned sky over encrusted silos :
heaven out on holiday,
past the silos, sky; the moth clouds slip to a wooded horizon
drenched in sap requisitioned fields

recipients to the blood troughs, garlands
of crimson. That is the suppercloth night. Gaper high
– This is the voice foghorning in the palmstalks
"Still buggering the geese?" the draught animals coated in fug
blackbird
rattling voice on the flagstones,
a sorrel headrest, the stale watercress

After the gale pylons got a new song.
Sling it, the old one was better.
Coils in furrows; earthworms
got there first shedding blue
raffia mud deposits

Robert Rosebud declares
moon's got sproutfields
to herself where pickers
gathered. One idiot fell
and bagged another's row.
You have done a fine trade in fools.

Wishes, screams, thus the convulsions of her child
splayed out, parachment pale
hands bow

Why stave off this work : it won't be done
at morning; it won't be done at all –
archeologist comes up coughing for air,
maggots, turtle grease crests his hair – he's pleased and

his work's done. Lie down. But why bother
with an ear of song, why lie down chaste
in sweat and thresh out stars; for you don't know
soup from salt, says the dream. Pebbles, bourne.

Nothing can wake you, no sound no lighted fire
the covers lie thick on your singing head
but your legs are bared, the pot is full : our Queen has
abdicated; winds lash windows with sticks, bones

lashes of rain cut into soil, twisting branches
of oak blow over horsemane grass the mercury left in

crushed oyster shells; nothing in your heart
nothing between our thighs will account for this

Bellows foam in the hearth : love possesses
this house instead of glass, floorboards spring
to her gait, too many windows
that could have closed, been on catch, lacked their panes

wind howled through plastic gashes, spread out sleeves
in the cob blew out fires made stoves smoke,
storms that gave you gutsache cut your lips
made you piss all the time made you unwhole.

No other life exists. Come in come in
out from the mosaic wind on thatch
Quick! from the crossroads, water splitting
galvanised rooves; come in fennel brow

for life is displayed here. Yeast ferments
in these walls. I've saved my news
for you, you saved your firewood for me.
Pull back the skewer, unlock this room

damp as a boat; grass rises behind the warp
in the pane, the bourne'll fill again
the song's logged with candlegrease
while our years cupcall past...

Spelt

... dismémbering | áll now. Heart, you round me right
With: Óur évening is over us; ...

What are these fears that emote themselves in the canvassing of a hiccup when people of Melanesian blood cross marble floors in Noumea? What does the phrase mean the gestural declension of blood is it to do with filleting of fish or what is the blood that comes to your cheek when you are running up the stairs and another is approaching how dare you shortchange me I demand at the very least to show impatience

I am quitting this island, I am quitting this continent with all I have appropriated in two in half, I think I will go through coy will go through the customs Declarations what 'ave I to declare I am richly a neutral I am neither French, Caldoche nor Melanesian, what am I taking back to the public when I find them I'll show them what's what and what there is to be eager upon

In this vein of connecting I have spent a lot of time with my cheeks refreshed by the sun and I am coming back to Europe with my cerveau full of the regal names of fruits and birds and hunting implements and flowers that you will never know what I am taking about which means you will impeach me in some lubricating way or other

Now that it is time for me to pack my valise of night and that the renettes the chiens bleus the other fabrications are not disturbing me now I can look back on this island and say I have not invaded a paradise where I learned a thing or two but not recalled how I could learn because I am uncoordinated dyslexic I am going to be epileptic and what is there but southern comfort from the peachjuice of the sky

Ah yes you remember my comfort you remember my cheek you remember my straying behind in the *case* while everybody went out looking for pommes canelles or checking the nasse to find the holiest most priestly lobster that there was was there more to say I stood under the cradle shade up there in the sky and I saw the pencement that battleship grey halfring in sky where the moon had been and raising my throat up to the post where my elbow was tendrilled and even and fair in any game of knuckles or leave-down-over I recalled I had copulated so often on this island and now I knew that I had learned something but you appropriated the abricot coloured paper shiny on one side in the bottom of the camping [trunk] my mouth was higher than yours last Sunday night that was ONE BLACK SLIT and this was another which you could shine against it would not hurt you gosh grace nothing would grab me I was far from my premonitions and presentiments Which body did I see run through with a thick knife before the weekend, and whose body was undreamt of below cherryblossom?

In the parc closed at one gate way where two men and a woman caressed each other a plastic caravan stood lit by what was encased by battery and generator and there was no watching sport or spring hooked up to their caravan it was more of A CONSTRUCT THAT SHOULD NOT HAVE BEEN THERE AT ALL and while I was walking through Noumea I discovered censorship did not extend to Gaston Gallimard and those whom his offspring published and stood there perusing Ernst Juenger Destouches *Le Livre Blanc* with the matelots' dicks spurting roman candles I especially liked that two handed book Marguerite Yourcenar's Fleuve negro spiriteuls Robert Desnos Max Jacob William Apolinaire when I read Ap I realised browsing was preferable to perusing and meant robbing but I was not in a mood for shoplifting I had other situations to get to grips with and that way the sun gave way to appearing for a little longer and I went to the Musée Canaque I knew that there were only weeks at most until people would endorse vigilantes and there would be lynchings animosities and trouble for the police but I did not envisage such a rhetorical blockbusting DELIVERANCE such as the G.I.G.N. taking out the hostages and executing them napalm and all why was this little stopwatch so dear to my heart made in Switzerland I was never going to get pretzels in this paysage

The woman's hair in the caravan oh yes we are back to that old storey that former novel if you like it I can arrange for you to have the author come to your terrasse and play you at noughts and crosses just to get things underway

The woman's hair was crowblack and heaped at almost the perimeter of her breasts, her back was small and covered although you could see sporadically her spine was teak

One dying and three living: a liverish quality had you been consuming quantities of silver foil butter shipped in from Normandy "where were you father on Saint Crispin's Day?" "down the pub" it would heartburn you frying on wooden planks this liverish qualitie took possession of blue green fields and allotments decayed plants and small parrots haphazard birds you know what is meant by keeping a stare on[1] and affiliated the reflections to those that are ricochet proof

1. 'Showing a stare'.

this caravan has a clammy-to-the-touch presentiment but a hectare or two of decomposure will do no good in the long term but for the short edit it is a viable form of blotting paper

Sun lit down on all pollutants of the river they do not require inventories you can guess
chutes pipettes and seepage

Your silhouette obroamatic gesturing with your lungs sieving full of air on a Silesian causeway
just down the steps jut to the left thassright sssh I am out snaring in the tribu this is the this is just the endeavour an endorsed method of Assembling informatique – dont overlook that when you've demobbed my scathing particular One I do see foam around the head and lips purple bruises on the sternum pass me your stethoscope I am a beginner I gaze through that tube oh it is so big is that a borehole a hole for your vantage they'll do luxuriantly fine as the barometer goes up bashful your silhouette reaffirms and tumultuous cliffs of FLOURESECENT AEROSPACE hanger-pleasure the colony polling booths must surely disseminate from in the glands oh this much is true you distress-call me with your lymphing arm broken in that position ist possible to fracture 'in so many places' don't be coy describing me your pleasures – I say it is richly pleasing to inhale vapours than just drink and swallow you shall soon be airlifted out of here it is not human form but hyaena and Alsatian who shoal at helicopter launch pads not who but 'that' snarl because BEASTS do not have the equivalent possessive I can assure you that my mouth has been forced open be installed and gulping about that

Eel Earth

a ray yal mis yel
owp cill ley yawp o prow
a ray medieval mise
yell-ed owlp sill leyline laugh

prowd a ray of fruit began
from fire eil aepe eel le
ept gatte post snowbrawn
hoy hoy ae lab hur sill go Tinker
out to see thi snow rub yor fore
                   head in it
                till it smart llit
bar now hit ees tuary
           eels hoy hoy
braun snowgape
             metal post prow
Tinker Labhur
Tristan

the sea cuffs earth 'n'
orchard
plovers gull and kelp
    what I hav to say .
        what I har to say
I here   I use my ears

hearing you plovers black green   c(rest)
          heraldry to drip vipers on any ambush

thank the kestrel drop lui, naguere si
beau, qu'il est comique et laid!
their ferry they'd sue Tinker Labhur
gills ees pord what I have to say

erc
gills ees pord what I hav to say
I err I rest in orchards
thi ease tie reat
chards cherts choves
charnel plovers   lugs and lulls pellmell
what I have to say don't drip on me
look at orchards
mist and airbrine earmilk
hedges cough

acute   /aconite fulcrum. Carnival endstops. Lavers and seaweed.

P.B.   a ripe green text (got that?) t   ex t . Ha.ha.ha.ha.ha.   Ho

You cannot desist. soitgoes. What waz good exactly conc. ian hamil

                ton finlay's work and mind an' campaign (19

42-

  O U T

meagre epoch rich meat floating on the sea;

look at Ballam's ass! Look at th' drip of limescale

+ red check Kurt's. Yaller gash on ciel ling, but cloc

duh dah duh Done? De nada =

Less flesh on limb or braid this plate. Earth to earth

vroom

 sembler à   /wasps smear down here

reign raid

Lines thru honeycomb Night swing see under vierge fulc ful fulcrum

                         .Layers' text stood out some.

Clean deposits rid of history. Time untouched by no more layers. Dust essent

ially untouch'd. o hermetic sediment. z. Text order left Competitive

caroline bergvall

FLÈSH

according to St Teresa of Avila

Do you suppose a person in perfect possession of her senses feels but little dismay at her soul being drawn above her, while sometimes as we read, even the body rises with it.

Things had been going Rather-Well. Sex-loot. Caravans of PushpUsh. Needy machines Easy To Please. pissabout reFillable. Everything pruned happy as shaved. Rubbed A Fff in it long Enough to Suck-off-Thereafter the stakes we'd lie in about. JUMPs the Surf with a Start. Off the ace Now-caught in. The Grip Of. Hot and tired. Row and row. Oars dig holes in Every Single Pie own I had ed absent-mindedly. Torn in the bell heat Kicks-Up spare-heads. Something's knocking against the SKin. large persistent bulks In the Air. Brutally pulled innards. Gut seizure GONgs concave

FLÈSH

according to Unica Zürn

As millions of blood corpsules desert her as the countless reds spots of an allergy cover her body she writes in her Manuscript of an Anaemic * :
"someone walked inside me, crossing from one side to the other".*

Red-folds a lot of bl. Bright deed. Dead Trance. Who will Carry The Stuff spews out of the Cave In. Having the Outline or surface Curved like the interior of a circle or sphere. What ddoesn't. Exhaust itself on Waste aWay on Contact. Engulfs the Surf's Being Lifted Up To. The Mouth of the Rover Banging under the skI. Explosion heats flans etc. Catches G cold on Entering-rbit. On The Face Of It's nothing mined leads to The Most disturbing The Most proFound Apparitions. Always a Throne stow away from knowing which of the Tears Profusely the Ho the Mo st

FLÈSH

according to Hannah Weiner

over the hill oh sometime myname
I was delivered from it

Reaching Inside a. Her bod Y retrieve Small lastiC ups. Meat is carved all over th. Her Insides. Bright were the. Daze. Pushing -error For The Sake Of T secretes (incessantly). P ushing The Boot If full corpse out of the. my her. Tackle. A Mouth-of V. draining Anatom Looking Around Actively falling-For I was Getting Into Bod. Y thinking this Giving Space might Temp For the Corps du Body for the Body of My Coeur. For the Coeur du Core du Corps Body Another WalkIn. Deep In The Hole. Such a Great ! Big irl of a Ho. Sleep wahwah walking. L- Holds. Rare attentions to abandon

FLÈSH

according to Kathy Acker

I write in the dizziness that seizes that which is fed up with language and attempts to escape through it: the abyss named fiction.

Who held Girdles wooed Held the Contemplative To Hand that which I'd take for Genuflections I take to genuflecting Takes me by the Keel-Over Busts my Hopen Fans Out like a Muscle. Edible bivalve mollusc. EBb Reast lights the Premises Maddeningly live-matter feels no Hate no L Go Figure s envisage a clea beach r coast nodal m odes d'efacement. Entire circuits tRipping on friction. A Face slow ed right-down revs the Grooves of Gyration comma the Stitching of Thought comma the Very Temporary Safety of Skin. AStride alights L- Keeps. Hail. In-Mouth Vegina

rajiv c. krishnan

The Progress

And this was when the night
  was black without being coloured.

Out of the mouths of coat-pockets,
                fingers of ginger,
  crawling underneath the soil of dank gloves

    came,
    guiding the hordes into the
     vicinity
                    God
                save the man
                        whose chest
                        contains her
And the loud thorn,
                cord and
                crick;
And tears are to cry with;
  and rhubarb and nettle make good soups.
The tautologous cruelty of roads,
  and the secret place of the joints
                crackled dryly at the stinginess
        of bags and boxes;
The euphemisms of loam:
        mosquitoes, gnats, octopussies,

and the crocodile of the Nile
and we came into an inaccuracy shouting:

Stevedore, first of all
load the hold with
ballast,
ink,
king and
orphan.

Kennel songs hovered
around the tight edges of analogies:
Man delays:
for printers lose their senses every day
precisely and carefully.
And tears are to hear with.

To go to bet to be:
dams, catchments, bunds, anicuts,
and the fields like starched pages
irrigated by giant hieroglyphs.

What else is noteworthy
is said to be an elephant.

And veder the weather will sound
                  xylophones
or emancipate yaks or zebras of the tundra
        or not, the continent of words
             floats before it sinks,
                  having ached after ink.

Lightly

(for Fiona Campbell)

The weird season of sickness
            throws down everything below
               beneath under:

The torment of parts and sides,
  weights and pressures, the feet
                weeping thro' bandages. Let
  eyes thaw, clocks grow, cats mew, for
   the wolf's maw, crow's craw, holds bills
          and bliss, roses
                nor green nor blue
That can gargle, worrying movement
               with its walk.

And you, eightmonth liver
        of the right kidney, you yet gallant
            iron gallotannate paper, trace
                    hesitations of tense, make but
blocks and stresses: lending, mending,
                bending, spending;
pushing, scratching,
                        smoothening out:
there are no more
            thesethings anymore; no more
braveries of incoherent storms,
    satisfactions of mowed lawns, softish
                baluster bushes
        argosies at yuletide. Across
    tiles grown yellow with lichen,
                    the whittawed skin
    bearing the white impress of truth
    as between the trees of life; and you,
                sow and litter
That will not turn brute in the fall,
            will be stretched.

And the kookaburra, that makes you run now,
    will surprize you with
            things and the sense they make;
Light among enemies, and
    as to foxing, wormholes and frass,

in spite of gutta-percha, bolts
nails and headbands
as firebrats and silver-
fish, below the social skin, will eat paper
if to liking.

And your places,
their ostentatious certainties lost,
shall desert be,
though bearing the folded gatherings.
That shall die, though
it body is,
and all that pother:
the sun on the wholly coast.

For water is another country
that lies down among herbs and villains.

Watches

(for Kate & Nigel Wheale)

These planes, spreading beyond courage
                into space, make noise,
        even in winter

  not as that terminal gravity, its
                    addiction to depths
        the ability to sniff exaltolide

  nor the microwave background
                prospecting for choice
across tic and stutter: provisory scars
    of time that saves daylight,
the available, the flamboyant, the only the

And get up
    to privations of sense
    to wrong forms of address
    to stealth and precision surgery
                    and sits on them;
                frightens oil—
            to be
        without walls:
    warmly is fleshly as lonely

Robin
Robin
Dustbin picker.

Even biodegradable brutes
                                        whaleswatch:
    only transients go in for mammals
The lineage of nostalgia is common
  tasking, accessible to detours.

To found upon ruin
    that radical poverty that is final
                kindness, as graphite that smiles
        on coppers and topers, as onions
            that scale Jacob's ladders:
a future in skies; but weeps—

nevertheless, something
                        to put into stockings.

Moonstarers
                to love ruin
                            sit not at ale bars
                new moral hit:

                    being anagrammatic

We run out of things
      of sense
      of O
   we're in that country now: first a

   wee bit wet canned sun;
   star was born: cook soon, burn later.

helen macdonald

Simple Objects

Not to touch the glare that breaks, and climate,
broaching the heart
with a talisman of salt. What hurt could be poured

to a glass and swung to see the bells of heaven ringing
for my procurement. A possible scratch sets me free

Of the modern, hear & fit mystery
to something I have to spell with no

nation, ankle deep in the mark, fretless
mirage radiant and anxious to settle

not least in the ambient glare. Catalogue me
where safety fits an evening outline, soldiers

firing at silver & the fringe of the pale sky
a conference of dotage, dying into the arctic

Caritas hijacked, music pulled in there, scent
erased in the deep temperature. Gauze follows

the return of an observation at a lines' end
soaked with flint and knocked by reddish sympathy

music sweats acres of slight and damaged inches
squared by the arc and protection of open water

but just to miss it, by this much, slapped
by plastic, and the press gathering toward

a hand of violets and cirrus hacked
backward to the infinite recession

of philosophy; that cloudy horizon
formulae of classic narcoses.

Act after act the spate is overdone
in a pyrrhic dusk, though the narrowing

of both eyes seems perfectly attained;
making mouths from the glass

white sleight of viper & file
whose past becomes a logic

spliced to itself and limited
only by the pressure encoded

at the neck's back. Putting
brevity at the angle of heel

and lake, halcyon days to pleat
in crape and claimants, all of them

felt and left and dressed in tactical red, readily
touched by high voices and a chancery dance

which whitens charcoal & leans hush against harm
so the throat broadens into song

here we are again
happy as can be
all good pals &
jolly good company

never mind the weather
never mind the rain

we weather tragedy
but the weather
is not tragic

off we go again

Material where the gallows
pillow & silence is

where the cloud gets
to fetch light & matter

meaning not a minute
waiting for a morning

I am alone and calm
beneath the juggled volumetrics

of hope and russian vine
minting water in a tier

of modest cause

to put the word here
where the mind was.

Occlusion of light
and sound left a space

for the matter, mere
havoc. At last, the token

gesture of trust. A grey space
uninhabited by fuss

Thereupon a nerveless mention, & through it
the tensile maceration of a copse-bound wind

hard enough to scrape four walls together
& wind up belaboured with years

uncomplicate in a heap, the years lie
uncomplicate in a heap

Small Hours

There is a brick in the cloud
              but it is not falling
it is night falling
is it true accomplishment breathing

The sky isn't blue not thinking
for days thinking for you

generally a small kind of bird looking
for premises
and they say the best is, yet
              to get near it

requires such fabric of years there is a
stroke through it
& I can stand on the pantomime wall
describing figures.

And above
a splint of mild lightness that is not
light at all that is all there is to love

Phosphorous

The curb is dead; half one hour
at the hospital gates with versions

corollary: the beautiful insulatory
properties of the English Channel

waning with imitative desires, wounds
at best shedding operative phraseology

along the coast, some hydrous shimmer
of silica and humorous mettle; love

in the mouth. He sorts her throwaway
lines & shouts in a fumy kind of translucent push

as demonstrations of thisness mesh into black-
edged letters & slated rings. If someone

or other inmate trembles this sleeping mean
to the manner of Davy's beautiful ice, not

wanting to replicate the dubious conditions
despite the need for water - when three

elevens construct a scalar height, one on one
to view the drift of a popular song & climb

to take the swarm from the sleepers breadth
then longing folds all fields to bright lines

and broadcasts heavy bunching too,
Such a beautiful delivery as a war is.

Tuist

I

Pleat the grounds they have scripted
as such, plus plumage, quiet lunches
on the hotel lawns slipping forward
'til we sense some dutiful square
and stop, pulling the whole rueful shore
to a ha ha, a net around practical ankles
    ah, how the hay smokes
into papaverous skies
as we address the heights of the C20th
in a poplin shirt, all declamatory and tired
with a suit that seals to rest these soft
and perfect metals. The organisation
owes everything; is fit to tweak
a neuralgic scene reading Auden
beneath a naked sheet in stormy cupolas
where the coupled latch and larchlap twitter
breaks sleet print through the cigarette
dries trays of warm roses & vocable ash
as hands permitting a multiple
sleepless walk for the uninked signatory
through august hours, the graces
who imagined that body of angels
and the debt before news, or words

as arms at the imprecise station
whose aim I cannot choose, being
a directive of squares
and breeze, tunnelling beauty
recovered & squired for the journey
briefly thumbing the air or worse
peripatetic squirms, nerves in nature
identical colours. That name at the firm
window is working effacement, soft gaps
and abstracted pairs to replace a miraculous
        slang with cramp
reparation of gifts and speech in repose
over waving clouds and malt skeins
a salt cheque, bruised with an isolate nuance
where a girl in the hand is worth two
in the lunular dust, supposing
a plus might emerge in the dark like a mouse
dyed strawberry blonde, a russet cup
with leavened blue stretches, a blue
from the bolt to cut that darling crop:
black light amounts to a bulb, the map
is a cognitive station amounting to dark
as a matter of course, brings
theories of crisp summer use
to be closed on the family hearth
that book beneath another burns
in birds and stipes a human heart

pricking out heartsease and fumitory
whose Troy, etc., and an operatic tremble
thinning widthways on powdery wires,
should kiss the choir searching for water
                    & seasonal coyness
funnelled up in the glistening hide
for comparable pleasantries. Hereby
some clouds drag above motion, dry
windward with westerly lime & hang
their dripping heels with music;
this surfeit proposes a well apart
from softness and leverage; songs
to stall and wake. A personal
historical waive is planning to do so;
steal a face slams a song in my heart.

II

    several lines to make
   a linnet who did not know whether
      he was a bird or no sleep
   in a cupboard grows to slake
      practice trills with a rattle
                    of fire

III

What means this, but soft
as a winged quail on turf [glut]
several spots of aeruginous blood
[but for] an accent, perfect
as a swerve from congeries to fear
from nothing to fear, from flood [damn]
to recoil from the heard response
& its demonstrable superfluities
to demolish the rails amidst [kilter]
recurring spoils in the eyes, to stand
on any difficult mountainside [again]
and the manner of features
the mutable hammers [reprises]

IV

Or mimics sleep to sleep
and so sleeps all for love
where a voice parades a handsome
faux-naif on stones. Clinker, clink clink
binoculars trained on Maeterlink, the
headland, the bobolink & the lyre

a great light I don't know over land nor sea
is colouring fires, looking down on the spilt lyric
to create the corporeal panegyric amid waste
peregrinations of speech and, so far as any
limit blushed with the weight could I get
an urban syllogism stapled in there yet

it was better *now*. With a rope
ladder falling from the golden
bough, warmly engrossed & gone
to seed legislature, she showed
anew great prescience, relaxing
in to enormous strictures, shuttling

miles out & up into fearsome
clouds whose lapse rate reaches
for calm. *Enter spring*
water & dreamt calculations
burned on the chest, since the least
whistle curling away from speech

where a helpful confluence of air
and alula sends accuracy up from its perch

in golden scales & cries *oriole* for rainbird

The New World

Memetics are mute phylogenies and smarting.
What is a hand for, but to be held? It is raining

in Georgia it is raining all over the world
applause rattles from the pilot's beak in choppy

breves and *savoir faire* lost somewhere between here
and home where the heart is whatever. The light

is hard in departures & tightness of the chest harder
weak toxologies the accents of the dreams aren't murder

scene after scene ships demeanour with trade
sets a leaving tear on each cheek & fades

and says: this is a real blade, fifteenth century, Japan.
Or: a peculiarly Germanic form of armour, no holes for eyes

black all over, annealed, the frayed corporeal manner
as the mouth sups grounds, faults and folds the arms under

but the shade of your eyes approximates the blade's blued dorsal edge
indigent as the model's side or even air, seen from below

every moment describes some other music
and I cannot remember banality ever existing

Dale

The storm runs forth on several seas whose manner is
the hard edge of a clamber down gneiss with a split thumb
bald inklings of wonderment, sun and trenchant killing bumped
by wrecked spume and clearing the throat, to try and shout
into the wind. Pulled out like warm glass. Where should flight

Eight choughs and three children, singing to a seal's head
on the lee side of the cliffs, hair fraying, *he-lo, he-lo* diatomite
and rain, disyllabic chuckle as the corvids glean turf and turn downwind
pealing back a sheet of egyptian cotton new/vraiment class
bled into a strong silence, just equalled by watching

Thirty breakers cowling in diagrammatic vice-lines with shortening frequency
replaced by thirty more/the ferry aspect two miles out dimmed by light
in cloud and rolls of clean water scrolling down. There are fits of waking.
I am waiting, it seems, for the cliff's right edge, but it is turned down
into a fence: slack barbs in hubs and shelves of thrift. Nothing sells

Nothing sells about this edge but fragrance, when the eyes are closed
enough to tip the head away from the ledge and settle it in welsh mud
'this is how the Irish write, as if with their left hand' she said, as soft
as anything, and the frown was half-sustained astonishment, looking
out across the waves as if a clause, then down at the paper in my hand

nothing as matter as fact as dislike occurs either here or for other places
as worn, something to get to. I could hurry by in a parsimonious cinch
frosted umbellifers and wagtails in the flat wastes ankle-deep in water
thinking how it got here and confusing this with national history:
natural history arches its timbre uncomfortably: nine races of *Motacilla*

flava, four of *alba,* victorious identification through chalk and paste
sliding eastwards on the vicious gradients come the disorientated:
twelve with a broken neck beneath the light and scores in bushes
on the wrong wind for this bird, a miracle behind glass
discarded on reflection

Walking

Where. Why and etcetera. The head bows & nothing is.
Shielding the harm from further harm is harder than this.
Voile & velux and little owls calling through dawn
mate selection, early spring on ash fence, white dots
a clave dancing sweetly on the posts. Not a call to arms
but I'm shaking anyway, and the sweet dawn is when
the wind gets up, half past four, cold on my face in the barn
in the sense of a register only: still alive, still hurt, whatever.

I am valorous in the face of such kindness, as ravens on pylons
stock doves and the roll of limestone bulks out our version
ripping out a throat in even dreams, eyes shut & breathing
concentrating on the sodden lake of the heart, and its sharp depths
up for retching on sweetness: sugar, tunes, airs, the memory of love

And a regular life. Where calm comes is never known, either
for the variety of declensions appall. Such a simple action alone
displacing a number of primary concepts, as trust and kindness
to dust, water: a lake of sweet cloves and lotus & the wind from the east
draining the land into raw salt and a poverty of sand and judgement
and I am balanced on one foot, assuming the next step is groundward
but wherever the ground is, blood.

Monhegan

The option presents itself & it is the geometry of behaviour
weakness addended as lists with a curious shear from the first
whet drawn to light and hurt is blessed with a broken wrist
law resets the amplitude and cuts the bias/is what the test

in overalls, taking a flip over the board like a run/line down cadillac
erred, forgiveably, damped down with a fluster of american thrushes
weak passerines dumped in a fall on an island dripping with monarchs
no headway against an easterly wind dropping on shingle and oxidised wrecks

the illness is on, and the curl of shot-filled waves pronounces a dare on deck
happy as I am, ready to pan back and take in the Kent house and a roll up to pines
scratching some lines on a rock with a peripheral cinder is fetching
collaboration of lures I wonder. First, second, and third year gannets

distinguishable by the distribution of hues. The patch of black
falls into the open eye like the bird into surf and sets up a ratchet
mechanism the wind and land dries the cornea and the sea's
slack tangent catches you like a tune & you turn, to sleep surely

in blue and red with salt in your hair and a pin in the throat
lacking/distress as a suite of biological fitness and lax finesse
handing us on to the museum, the ice house and the light
house stilled by environmental occurences whenever/the gut carved by nuance

as the merlins tip and fall into a carrying wind, scoring a sixty foot drop into
                                                                      starlings
and out into the channel below, chittering with satisfaction or annoyance or fear
turning to present eight toes to a conspecific rival image & the sky is darkening.
Where rate of change chanced to mark itself against a chevron of feathers

pushed by a proximate cause from Nova Scotia southward, eight ounces, six ounces,
                                                                      a curl
nowhere drypoint or the heel of a gull. What, here, is warmed onto palaver
by which the painter is searching for a rectangle of warm colour
linseed flat tactile slick on the instant and searching for a wall

Taxonomy

Wren. Full song. No subsong. Call of alarm, spreketh & ought
damage the eyes with its form, small body, tail pricked up & beak like a hair

trailed through briars & at a distance scored with lime-scent in the nose
like scrapings from a goldsmith's cuttle, rock alum and fair butter well-temped

which script goes is unrecognised by this one, is pulled by the ear
in anger the line at fault is under and inwardly drear as a bridge in winter

reared up inotherwise to seal the eyes through darkness, the bridge speaks
it does not speak, the starlings speak that steal the speech of men, *uc antea*

a spark that meets the idea of itself, apparently fearless.
Ah cruelty. & I had not stopped to think upon it

& I had not extended it into the world for love for naught.

peter manson

The Ice Skaters

They blithely lurch during the downcast transparency,
Fir corners contra snow-imminent empyrean engraved
Well pull, curvet, chassée, and decline

Blithely away – an age deduct, this occasion. I discover them
Lustrous blonde and burnished cryptic and girlfriend-
coloured engage, abscond, spin, and away additionally

During the easy firm luster. Inferior their legs
Spinning also blithely what abysmal estate reside
Of cryptic or marijuana or retarded fool poking former,

What essence-curs of roil, what entangles of marijuana –
They decline during the rise beckoning us along,
Cautious we ensue, experiment the defense – excellent,

They demand, lurching absent blithely. You
Adventure against dupe them up, gain eject, and
Discovery yourself trying pull black drool. Demand,

Ice pull your face, sputtering dully, defeat,
Defeat to the roil, perplexing for marijuana you die.
Their laughter jingles skillfully during the ice.

after Philip Hobsbaum

Summer Sadness

The sun runs a lazy tub in your hair's goldness,
Fighter, asleep on the sand,
And, burning incense on your traitor jowl,
Folds-in your tears to a love-potion.

The changeless lull of this white blaze
Has made my timid kisses say in sadness:
     "Never shall we rest, a lonely mummy
      Under the antique desert and the happy palms!"

But your hair's a lukewarm river:
A place for drowning, coldly, the soul that haunts us
And for finding this 'Nothingness' you do not know!

I'll lick the shadow from your lidded eyes
To see if it will lend the heart you batter
The insensibility of the stones and sky.

from Mallarmé

Sarin Canasta

Clock's Dog: How stupid do you feel
and how stupid can you?

Mrs. Tungsten Loop: King Ilona, your rapport / portable
Intake valve recovers. In clover.

King Ilona: Lemon residue, shan't I be
the relict, Mrs. Tungsten Loop?

Residue at one eight oh
Celsius.

Clock's Dog: It must age, select ramparts don't
foundation garments closed to secure tree-bark

Not Amity, deflect method, refine
the length of a hare, what won't you seize up

Bedded here / a nation closer
again, this herbery.

King Ilona: Ravenna is all hair.

Mrs. Tungsten Loop: Amen.

Clock's Dog: The region before the ventral part of Calum
is fluidised by an air-blast

I cannot describe. Sarah is saying No.
Jennifer as a trope cleverly sanctioned

	Extends on a leaf southward to the tongue of Ross. Neighbours of Steven exempt Cathleen.
Mrs. Tungsten Loop:	That this, in historical time might subtly reanimate fear, seems
	a long shot.
King Ilona:	How little like the human mind anything
	is, and how much like a brain.
Mrs. Tungsten Loop:	The face facing the back of your face moves to distinctness with sunrise.
Clock's Dog:	Don't ever let me exist, will you?
King Ilona:	This is the time of incubation.
Mrs. Tungsten Loop:	How many years to hatch our imbecile?
King Ilona:	The lamps are on, we are in wool, the cameras roll.
Mrs. Tungsten Loop:	This is an event, somewhere.
Clock's Dog:	But too many boiled in the shell, leaving the compound freak uneven
	and liable to eat its parent.

rob macKenzie

Taliban lamp-post

The stoor, enjambement, drug'n shop
suggest it's more'n a teuchtar's first trip south
excites the four-track shock;
the Cortina loafing through the loose estates.

Solid's a Seventies side-burn. Dura-plastic.
First stereo confluence – inter-roped Maghma and Pedma,
Country *and* Western –
though, in the end, the sentiment's more durable than the kit.

Encapsulating loons, the four-track's engineers.
Cassette came – little, shiny, rewindable –
an' vinyl keeps its kundalini charm.

A teenage ascendancy then, short's my own
short trust in th'infinite community.
Three days in Edinburgh.

Toffee Bó! The latest Highland free-gifter.
Mother for giving in us all; rock for taking.
Enquire after Leverhulme'r Redland.

Now privatised, post-empire, the creep'n snap'f
our common subduction's
some corporate division. But, being bardic,

there's a poem in it at least.
"Gur ann an Ameireaga tha sinn an drasd'
fo dhubhar na coille nach teirig gu brath."

Well, it sure proved a short forever
an' all the poet sees's the footprint never made.

Ca'l an dànachd air am buaith?
Or, better yet, on the line escaping victory an' loss?

Like Pruppacher, Angell an' Bartell's
snagged on the properties of water.
T_s's th'asymptote to all derivative properties –
c_v, c_p, α_T –
where the ghost liquid finally gives up.
But two percent of solute
an' God's in his place, Hamlet on his linear throne.
Some short extrapolation hives off
th'anomaly an' the remainder's
normal as any Winchester. Which is as well,
when, expanded supersonically, condensation's
to the liquid, as far below T_s
as itself below freezing. Taliban spring.

Lamp-posts in leaf w'tape an' beardless men.
Faith xerophyte as heather. Familiar
as a Sunday supplement's Lewis.

Conduct the following dream:
bake a continental loaf – white, floury,
liable to melt in mouthfuls –

but leave it out. It'll spoor in shadow,
castellate in sun. Save
your compassion, it's bread.

Wonder what Communism could've achieved
beyond fifty years of peace, re-dress,
bureaucracy an' death. It's gone,
and without the fighting which,
could there've been, who'd've picked the sides?
Would International Labour've fought
for itself, or some system
as far beyond a singularity of paths
as the Sharia spring?

The phase space dells're filling up
like so many weary politicians' eyes.
That not zealous in us learns the absent truth.
Our patriotism, socialism, christianity,
libido, hunger and theory of chance flutter.

Our involvement knots, breaks and streams:
there is, after all, sleep, journeying

in the unblinking colour of earth.
Dè tha fios againn airson dubh an taghadh?

Nurbibi means lady of night
even waist deep in dirt, an' black
w'blood from stoning.

Adultery means t'approach one another,
even when that other's breaking you
into an untidy pyramid.

' Bit datastream in hard millihertz;
never laugh at that old BBC again.
Eye the ROM suspiciously;
there's blood on the tape drive.
An' maybe slower is better –
even Americans kill slowly when they mean it.
Collateral damage, Sparky, equity
an' the Shopping Channel pay
f'r the speed of light's packaging.

In Afghanistan the unwound trees
attract a symbol'f my experience:
every self of me rickling unconditionally
like ribbons of under-milked tea;
like the inky trickle'f fluid dynamics

wraps its false-colour filaments round geophysics,
curlicues, then breaks.
Not without worth. Gaia's below the grid,
and information. But fouled're friendship,
hope, gaelic an' ambition – all it fails itself.

There're two forces for growth:
supersaturation's radiative heat loss – trial and ease –
i'the crystal growth'f ice,
an aghaidh tri resiostoirean: diffusion'f heat,
likewise mass, 'us surface kinetics –
àm air an locair
a rannsachadh an sniomhanach –
an adatom-sized sweat an' rain.

The crystal grows; fault remains the same.
Archimedes 'n Escher laugh uncontrollably,
but only if the playground's bigger than the game
an' the rain's a drizzle. Simple
in the lab, but in the earth's sense?

Here flux's are'n flux
waves dissipate
an' all our measurements ask

should gaelic live?
Kirk aye, toun no, schule tint.

Duendishly prepositional, spectral,
more regular'n english,

though there's no length of learning
lets you talk with your parents.

Chan e "Dè gaidhlig a th'air x" ach
"Dè a tha gorm'sa bheurla?".
Teip gu teip.

Precious metaphor. The tape-tree's mine,
bought with license, 'r acquiescence to advertising.
Sold b'that predication'f belief
'at's Nike's negative religion.

The fundamentals hardly ever change.
And when they do, we buy our identity colours
for crisis. The cones o' glaur must gi'es pause
like Pepsi them. So far away. So lingual.

Fight your good fights.
Let he who is without synthesis
cast the first stone.
Festoon the lamp-posts.

Comfort for the Revd. Angus Smith, Ness

'f there was rain, flat black Cambridge'd
bubble and flake like varnish, leave nothing
but an expert nomenclature, pink suspensions,
and some algorithmical solace.

I doubt you see it a collapsed Edinburgh,
minister, lacking the sheer colleges, sharp
etiquette for grace and nothing
beyond High Table falsification, nothing revealed.

Stony ground for revival when the Sunday ferry
sails even toward Stornoway now?
A camel's hope for Cambridge if even on Lewis
the coves slop out'f The Narrows Friday night?

I'd've agreed, among the yellowing accents, until I fell
in with a midsummer woman, labial ring,
dreadlocks and cotton, scarf-collared dog and
everything about her careful and dirty and painted.

'far from the South as a childhood
on the island: subject to draughts, strong beer,
peculiar convictions. She's reconstructed
a village from her own faint sense of it,

for most of the world like Ness
in the 1960s
(if short of the kirk and guga and fine football team.
For all that an island, convex like Lewis).

You were a high tower then, minister, in 'sixty five
when you stopped traffic, turned the tide of Skye ferries.
The precipitate rhythms in your voice
beat back the supercilious timetable:

I desire to go to the ferry on the Sabbath day –
to stand or sit or lie down – to be a barrier,
and theology fell like a log in front of the lorries,
toppled by a culture with the post-modern

in its pouch like tar, ready for the stump.
It's rigid, and pointless defeat, then, but
only on that one shore, minister, only
if we allow their theory that all we have

is an empty Sabbath. And only if we'll not
look up and see the blythe-bidden opportunity,
the new travellers and the disassembling South,
the new congregations of love and morality.

Comfort for Ferrier

We're on the last blunt headland home,
sucking mints, it gone eleven
and tomorrow Sunday. Hard-by me Finlay
the fisherman's ablaze, cross the aisle's

a Mason winking. In front, a Moderator
of the Lord's third millennium annotates the air
in a salmon farmer's breath, losing, for once,
on the point of transubstantiating faith.

Some irony, that here's the crucible
you thought lost when Edinburgh's moral chair
turned evangelical! Natural enough then,
in 'fifty-two, your lack of grace towards

those *parrots in their ignorance, worse
than parrots in their spite*, who'd best be *nailed
flat against the doors of every philosophical class-
room* in the land. And many's the trope

has sprung since yours from that slip
of the drifting Scottish mind,
crows behind the teeth
of MacKay Brown, Muir and Crichton Smith.

But now, bright now, in it's last true hand,
the *absolute blade*'s proved keen for education,
at that speculative, not hacking down
the *starving haulms* we may sometime have been.

The islands fuel universities, and
if there is some anaerobic *undersong*
of terrible holy joy, what crop's above
but democratic intellect? Lewis

is the wind's feature, and the sea's, the flushed
conch at Scotland's ear.
                    By me, Finlay's hand
is big and hard from work; mine's soft and small
from algebra, Marx, and the struggle with the word.

air falbh

Brìde nan casan geala an' her lye-milk beach-dried known tomorrow.

Brìde na cruach torach, agus a fior-ghlanadh torn
peat flank coat heavily enough and herself gone.

fear dhusgadh nan crèidmheach agus na crèidmheach fhèin
o' the fused operative kine mouth state.

fear faire Chrìosda hengit crack-necked instance o' death
food an' corporality morning b' morning dew t'awake.

the whole but internecine bull-calves na h-òige.

Little Austrian boy crying Mammy

To see him clack an end to the pirouette
that loses his mother in the lacquer
Hapsburg made of art flushes my stomach

and heaves on the tendons in my neck.
Panic sucks the wee boy into his bladder
and mammy disappears from my own gallery

(which is in Glasgow). My cold
stomach floods. He clutches at
his tiny cock. Art and families

smack the walls like ivoried gas.
I understand the paintings.
We are both regained.

A punctuation ghetto for

, comma, comma –, full stop
,:, semi-colon ":-:, full stop
":.,?, full stop .;.:", question mark
lip mark .,:? lip mark ":
.,!: comma .,:.;,?, full stop
,: em-dash ":,?,?, question mark em-dash
-,:., hyphen,, full stop .;, full stop, fullstop

'Se jazz a' bhaile bh'ann
snug i' the cusp 'tween

Cold War Chaos an' the ceilidh
Jahweh brickbat ballets

on the Castle's appropriate lawn
the sad day gone we left the croft

an' the old rebellion began
Union Jack thalla's cac

two fingers to NATO, the cuiream,
agus pompous American Rock

just three chopped chords an'
unavoidable lilt le clachan ùr

Lewis Punk bands of the early 1980s

Off Ardglas

The sea's some kind of grey off Ardglas, the air
and the sky're giving up height on plates. Left,
Stac Geal has the widow's swell on
and a lapful of china from the light. The rocks've
gone some strange loose flesh colour with the gulls.

You know it well enough, Ardglas, the spur
single-tracked and the ribs fenced. See
the bearded cars white-settling, sheep in closed
session, children trading cigarettes and saliva
in the lee of the Free Church manse?

Here's lazybeds collapsed and a mattress
of potato. Here the awkward oilskin's caught
only itself on the byre hook, dripping pullets,
and nothing has the time of Murdo's loom.
Something of my forehead's in the scene.

alison flett

Time and Again

thi cloak
oan thi waw
sesitz timety

get thi bairnz reddy
get thi hoos tidy
get thi messijis in
get thi tee oan
get inty bed
an gee um hiz conjuggles

thur wizza time when
I

naw thur wizny

Whit Lassyz Ur Inty

shiny paintid boaxis
wi wee twurly
twiddly keez
thit creek oapin
tay riveel

pink silky satin
an bitsy mirrur
an a toty plastic
ballyreena
rijid an frilly
turnin in surculz
oan thi wun spoat
in timety
a nice
wee
tune

lassyz rilate
tay aw that
shite

feerd

kizzy ast
firriz fare
a wee bit
too loud

kizziz ize
wur
lookn diffrint
waze

kizzy didny
wok strate
doon thi ile

kizzy lookt
it ivrywun
grinnin

ivry
singul
wunny us
stared
ooty thi windy

Dinny

a man oappsit
oan thi bus
cuddlin his bairn

no jist
that tite parent-hold
stop kickin
stop bouncin
turn roond
face thi frunt
holdin doon
trine tay keep still
bit akshul
cooried inty thi kid
cuddlin

an my god
there it wiz
in public too
a kiss
oan thi bairns cheek

a kiss
like a wee red flower
amidst thi flashin past

o blank shop frunts
an strugglin buggys
an bairns oan leeds
an stony grown up faces

mare outrageous
than a snoggin cupple
kissin bairns in public places

in this oor grey granite land
where the only way men have left
tay show their bairns they love them
is ti say
dinny day that (yill hurt yirsel)
an then
dinny day that
an then jist
dinny

Lettin thi side doon

christ
thi downward thump
o fist oan table
thi jump
an shivery
cup in sosser
(rinkulz tremblin oan skin
uv look worrum tee)

thi crack
a peerin
in ma voys
widens
thretinz tay let oot
sumthin nasty

sept fur rimembrin
(dispite hevvy Cover Up)
thi cashul swell
o ma blooish I
an looksy disgust
fay nayburz
an fay him

eftir aw
whit kindy wummin
pits up
wi thi sorty shite
thit shoze?

taking offence

he sayz
gawn hen
geez a feely
yur tits

ah sayz
awane huvva wank

or it leest
thatz whit
ah woody sayd
sept ah thot he mite be
uffendit

cock	tail
pit	off
ahoop	piece
aleeki	away b
e sure	oard g
crow o	ate sp
the wa	in wag
lk and	ging t
bull a	he dog
nd ball	between
s a snoo	the legs
k 's co	back pi
mb tea	ece of
ser	end

wee sparx

ah see yi ivry week
thi kewryus angully
yir foaldid arrum

thi wy yi
gulp
back fag smoke
an blow
puffin oot yir cheex

thi incline
o yir heed
when lissnin

laftur burstin
throo
yir oapin mooth

wee sparksy yoo
flickurin
in uthur folk

yir thare jist firra seckind
then bang
that stummick punch

yir deed

Ghost

this wummin
I

ah dinny

a wummin
wi hur brests
wi wun brest
hingin oot

ah jist dinny

oan a wee
scoattish island

ah dinny wonty

thi man
whay seen hur
thi man
whay came
oan a boat

no

thi wummin
an hur bairn
ma bairn
waytin alone
mibby thi last wunz
eftur an infestayshun
o rats
et aw thi crops
an thi islandurz
starved
tay deth

no

jist this wummin
thi man foond
oan thi shore
an hur baby
ma baby
hurz

ah dinny wonty

lyin
oan thi shore
thi bairnz wee moo
still clampt roond

hur nippul
ize starin

thur ize

starin inty darkniss

ah dinny wonty
think aboot it

Fat Lady Sings

ahm no
a skinny wummin
trapt inside
a fat wumminz
boady

naw

ma inner selz
way way way
biggurn this

ma inner selz
FUKN HYOOJ
wi big
JUMBLIN tits
nMASSIV
swoallin nippulz
nroals nroallsy
wobblin
tumblin
FAT
follin in foalds
downty ma
grate swayin buttux

ma soft
dimplin thize
ur splade
sayn
FUCK ME

ma soft
pudjy fingurz
ur splade
sayn
FUCK YOU

ahm dansin
an ma boadyz
dansin wi me
an aroond mi

whit yoo seez
jist
thi haffy it

Non Sequitur

thatsa loady pish

how kin yi say
am fuckn thick
jiss kiz ah dinny ken
whit a non-fuckn sekwitur is

thurs prolly hunners i peepul
dinny ken that
disny meanty say
thur aw thick

yir tokin bawlicks

wokkin hame

how glammurus
lit up
thi late nite bus

nestling

o
thi wee burdz
i
uv yoo

blinks deep
inside
uv me

an ma hole body
melts
inty softness
surroundin
holdin
protectin

waiting ankshus
fur thi day
yoo fly

Lernin

thi wummin iz standin
by thi doar
thi wee boy iz rite
inside thi shoap
thi man iz bitween
thi wummin
an thi boy

thi wee boy iz greetin
wi hiz hole body
thi wee shoodurz
shuddur
inside thi bobbly lookn
jumpur wi
sumthin sticky smujd
doon thi frunt
teerz make white scarz
throo thi muck
oan hiz crumply face

thi man goze
fukn MOOV
ah telt yi
moov it
NOW

thi wee laddy
greets hardur
mummy
he sayz
hiz arms reechin up
tay hur
mummy ah wont YOO
mummy PLEEZ

thi wummin
looks at thi boy
hur eyebrows rinkul
hur body twitchiz
taywordz thi bairn
then she stops
looks at thi man
jist yoo stay
rite thare hen
he sayz
ahv telt yi bifor
dinny giv inty him
thi boyz goaty lern
yi heer mi?
thi boyz goaty lern

drew milne

Satyrs and mephitic angels

Go litel bok, invoice these strain line shadow inks,
or suffer in silence imago mephitis,
I can smell your poison squirt of ingrained chalice,

squids in blood-dust of leavening slates, it blakes too,
or as art suffering dusts this its antique time
and that there monstrous word glory in suffering.

A dangerous demagogic word holds us surely,
like the masses the measure *is* suffer; for these
abolitionist crudités, as raw mangetout,

may smash up (*piano*) while your smudge spill barks out
beyond purely verstehenden explication,
in these hand sewn diagnostics of future past.

If as tool performed the so forth poises genie,
angle as massage stones of which the knights Templar
will build over geo-roof folie de patrie,

and not notorious dress codes of tea-room zones,
in memoriam tears torn in atomiser
stutter sprays: but which public takes this reading room

challenge to continuous administrative
contacts? We press on in class marks etching wretches,
we as two roles flush out imagoless twinnies,

touchstones plate these nail grimy as naught or nothing
under the optic sun: d'you know it too, lumpen
prole boho, all declassé like fat sump fury,

eh fairy with the awful smell glues mephitic.

Dolphin song

Would I were as Arion, or as the story told,
choosing harp fish swordpens to take the plank, the egg,
the swallowing passion in supperless *díke*.

Where is that dolphin now? we still adhere to the
doctrine of redemption which originally
connoted a slave purchasing his liberty:

not to change its world but to escape this, it has
flown off the wheel, off grief's thole misery while vine
sprays against are its expenses. For dolphin song

no season supposes such slavery orphic,
while urban revolution remains roused as lyres
for the hungry he hath filled with such good things, of

which one among is hunger *anánke*, potlach
expenses defrayed deformist, details lacking
as if normal proceeding will follow slaughter,

or our harmony parts dissolve clear and brittle.

Denizens of low street

All along the low street hopes akimbo, and plants
wilder but denizened out spit it, upon this
cobble sliding hurts all midlothian drag-heart,

while the mile's bilious rain *smiles better*, which now
castles into palaces we have not outlived,
and feels blood apocryphal drive the denizens,

vomiters, and *ye of scant hope* shuffling among
rucksack rashes, to wish some purdah for to be
and not notes on the decline of Scottish murder.

The Sappho parchment clasps our bitten horizon:
there is pornocracy, which no pibroch here sings,
just as still water runs deep swimmingly below:

pray tell, not calmly, to lease punctured yearning clans,
is it this way lies mercat ahoy festival;
go and Campbell it out along the soup high way

autobahn to Glencoe, while you stake the low roads,
I'll die before you, fit-you-saying speak-easy in
pop furious ballad style: *Warhol? I'll Warhol you!*

That lettre à d'Alembert misweighed how the
civic joy can be stationed for the tart riposte:
under three crosses mercat you can spot the ball,

here of all places, and you thrill to hideous
cork thrust damage remissness of *where I belong*,
as those in dicky birds drooping groove their night-piss.

That vamp still acts, dreaming eats of tourists for tea,
whose ghost con-tours will not bring back the silver birch,
and the cambered *pace* macadam rolls sighways,

while beneath, children pass for the well clad courtless,
playing private nursery courts in romper suits,
states streamed as united colours of brash refuge,

but *will the car be ready*, dreams wild one freezing,
still refusing the grim one bar heating cross road,
as residual rockbearing slough sudsiding cries:

Nova oh no Scotia, lime my sheepless north face.

Hibernations

The shadows are longer, out of touch with its times,
but the geese-steps of accommodation bristle
and are still life no more, you know the *kind of* thing;

O money, O function, O job, lend me just the
private and confidential, dazzled convictions
of the prevailing *absolutely wrong*, or so.

It's all over bar the accountancy and the
dispiriting fibre of the nevertheless
necessary reticence. Old hat, can I not

eat the psalms, the blushes, the feigned departures,
and then the kandym, perchance to skip from tuber
to tumour, abashed at the violence of critique

in toyish, dyspeptic, slow-grilled embarrassment.

from *A Garden of Tears*

III

Better you to me than I were to myself
but what water we were I'm against it still,
the turn on love is patience and thousand lies
while sleepless still loves we cannot sleep still with,
are breathless but still lives we cannot breathe with,
til doubt gives in fear and throws the first light stone
against names we never made, and loving break,
our breast plate of sighs in armour of accord:
call it operation bouffe, a taking leave
in lost of means, burnt islands and grimaces,
that's one end or two, a rash passion of notes
whose calm call shall remain nameless, but is law,
where wills are alive with the sound of water,
water of our eyes falling, felt and all told.

VI

Come in the valley of the shadow of breath
where we are this kiss in impossible grief,
that never savoured wrench as now and never
when happen is, the thinking over descant
to once upon each other, folded in sums,
parts in inconstant disarray of ice
as this scream is, an only shade of dismay
that pulls each faceless tooth along to wisdom:
these are our lines upon each blowing birth bruise
dashed to lungs, as skin curls in such heavy fruit,
its lisp already for that day when one dies,
simply leaves, or forgets the flares of always,
left flickering stunned in early fear of now
when each feared for kiss is still a greater death.

from *Aggropolis*

Worse is come under in
inclement skies, before
each dark spit takes you
to water felt upon awes,
dusts down in pig iron,
swan of arc-light, flock
done to sparry feather,
ember gorse in dolefuls.

In wet soil, crisp white
scale holds to its mire,
what drip stalks, such
cut swathes, the rumble
slump and insert larks,
its best lie deep, steady,
the number dogs do lay
a dirt trail in each script.

Blue moon on fed day,
smiles so still, or soon
dies, drops a halo, hot
suits of nuclear electric
on th'ensanguined suns,
garb o grime, in rails of
bleached bondehede, no
ash of its worth or page.

O fucked city, its agon
lustre in foamy rind, to
do so soft with then on
acrylic afternoons, our
one good eye flowering
me with disaffections,
ah mine hurt, it shrinks
from less, it shrugs on.

As bake or dearth into
star cot, let's lie lower
love, let's lie low until
no dark so comfortless
blight of agent can still
wager head against our
rotting core, as they do
expatiate of this or fall.

Have you left my ear to
locks, a field of night in
the mine, ivresse as this
hair kindles into meteor
or blows of die, a mark
as fur or as sark blisters
rent asunder, its moral
streaks in fiery blesses.

john kinsella

Verandah and Watermelon

This year's wheat cheque
and a remarkable yield
on sand plain country
accompany slices
of watermelon
on the back verandah.
A daughter calculates
debt per equity ratio,
her brother listens
to the cricket score
on the radio.
A parrot drops
a set of nectarines
with its bolt-cutter beak
and the farmer doesn't
even move. His wife
looks nervously at
the rifle and waits.
More nectarines
and he doesn't seem
to care. What about
those markets? What's
happening with subsidies?
Went sixteen bags an acre
of sand plain country.
Well I'll be damned.

Parrot Deaths: Rites of Passage

Blue clouds scuttle the eucalypt sun
as it fizzes and winces with impending
rain, sultry weather dampening
the orange hearts of king parrots.

The scimitar roads cull the golden grain
from dump trucks and belly spillers, tarps
tethered loosely, illegal loads shifting
over axles tense with excess tonnage.

Rosellas gather about the grain offerings
and the torn bodies of the fallen. Wood smoke
hustles a magpie lark out of an uncharacteristic
torpor. A crow hangs low and watches intently.

Observing the rites of passage a regent
parrot plunges into the dead eyes of a semi,
eyes of silver nitrate, tarnished and stained
shadow black. The orange, golden and emerald

hearts of parrots litter the roads. I drive
slowly and whisper prayers of deflection.

Miner

Despite a dozen hotels
I would continue past all, straight
to the coffee palace with its wood
and whitewashed hessian walls.

I was happiest when working the Cosmopolitan,
it being in the middle of the town
and not much travelling.

And the war stripped the district
clean to the bone,
and the few mines left open
worked frantically.

Miner's Wife

And then I caught the boy
floating in the red creek
in an old water tank,
though I left him to it,
it not having rained
for months.

And I said that if my church isn't good enough,
then I'll be damned if I'll go into hers.

And I left water
on the verandah
for the wanderers
of the desert
and respected
the spirits.

Pantoum

souwester blows cold
ha ha says granma
you'll chill to the bone
out there on the water

ha ha says granma
we gotta anyway
out there on the water
that's where goes sun & moon

we gotta anyway
cold when it oughta be hot
that's where goes sun & moon
burst & mix with blue

cold when it oughta be hot
we saw it in the telescope
burst & mix with blue
burnt dark like the road

we saw it in the telescope
granpa let us look
burnt dark like the road
& too close to lie

Tension Nut

He's the bastard
who'll knock a sheep's
eye out as soon
as look at it

Or drive his tension nut
repeatedly
into the skull of a lamb

Old McNaddy took him out
on the salt flats last week
and beat the livin' daylights
out of him

McNaddy reckons
doin' that to a lamb's
a little bit steep.

Death of a Phacalogyte

The cat'd delivered four
to the back door that month.
One was found submerged
    in its drinking bowl.
All male, it was guessed
they'd lost the strength
through coition, it being
common for ejaculation
    to result in death.
The farmer's youngest son
    reclaimed the corpse
    from the cat's bowl
and replaced water with
formaldehyde, the phacalogyte
surfacing limply during
'show and tell' at school.

Mala In Se: Death of an Innocent by Snakebite

Mala prohibita or mala in se? The snake bites
and withdraws undetected. Death comes quietly
some hours later, an assumed thorn penetration
becomes a major oversight. Three weeks back a young
girl died in just this way on a neigbouring property,
an examination of her vital fluids revealing the venom.

In weighing the heart against the feather a trace of venom
will upset even the roughest of scales, the truth bites
the axis, destroys the balance, claims its property.
So, struck down in the hay shed, youth goes quietly,
taking its time over dinner and television, the young
in body and mind ignoring death's subtle penetration.

It shouldn't be allowed they say, this penetration
of our lives – it's said by parent and doctor, the venom
tilting the balance in favour of *mala prohibita.* The young
girl's sisters are most vocal in this – living the bites
of snakes *in-stigmata*, cursing thorns as advocates. Quietly
time will soften bitterness and life return to the property.

But this, the fourth week since death claimed its property,
has not brought release. A red sun's harsh penetration
has not prevented an early winter falling quietly
though surely over paddocks, as fog in gullies, a venom

that is almost light and thin though deadly. Heat bites
like frostbite, the crow's glare destroys its young.

Mala in se someone actually mentioned – respect the young
came the reply (it was when the fallen girl's property
was being divided between her sisters). A tear bites
a stranger's flesh more than the knife – the penetration
of words well attested. So *mala in se* became a venom
more toxic than that of the snake. So, speak of it quietly.

We sit with the family on the ivy-clad verandah, quietly
discussing death and a cold sunset, the evening is young
though already a heavy darkness has set; but there is no venom
in the speech – acceptance from somewhere deep in the property
is slipping in: the call of crow and galah is penetration
enough to break bitterness. Cold though – even acceptance bites.

So quietly the soul retreats, no longer the property
of a sadness unwilling to release: the young soul's penetration
of *mala prohibita*'s venom. The lightness (*mala in se*) bites.

Where Soul Birds Sit

Where cats store the mummifying heads
of rare parrots
Where farmers destroy rabbits
with tubes of Phos-toxin,
Where bull-sized bellows lay useless
their leather stomachs strengthless
and decomposing   their beaks corroding
Where dead trees mark salinity
Where dams sit isolated in the centre
of paddocks collecting residues
Where dogs work sheep or live on chains
Where the wind cuts between two fires
burning towards each other   similarly
shaped and featured   sparking over
firebreaks ashen and the colour
of pumice, cockeyed bobs spiralling
flame from one side into the other
until all fuel is drained and the scene
looks pale and defeated
Where Soul Birds sit high over roadsides
or hover above fire
withdrawing deep into forest
with night   heads twisting the same way
as water twists down a plughole.

aidan andrew dun

from *Vale Royal*

the river knows the answer
and the way to go

In the trip of a star-crossed summer,
in the sadness of my disconnection,
I ran adrift in the city of exterior light.

I jumped off a merry-go-round of transience
and disappeared in the streets, saying:
Now let the good times roll.

I had lingered in the guidelines long enough,
and so without a destination, I set out,
not intending to turn back very soon.

Saying to myself: The sun is born at midnight,   10
I made the best of this idiot pilgrimage,
sleeping in the way-stations of flight.

In wide arcs of wandering through the city
I saw to either side of what is seen,
and noticed treasures where it was thought there were none.

I passed through a more fluid city.
I broke up the imprint of all familiar places,
shutting my eyes to the boredom of modern contours.

There were canals where streets had been.
And powerfully reflected light
obliterated whole ranks of unsuitable buildings.

Asceticism was my dream.
Disillusionment demanded no less.
I floated downstream with indifference.

My one idea was to stay outside
until everything but the indestructible
had been destroyed.

Astray in the void of connectedness,
I left behind past and predictable worlds
and span on a new axis out of sight.

And so I came to the place called Pan Cross,
and the Plain of Good Luck,
where the workers with golden hands

Are building the Cathedral of the Sunchild
beside the river, on the cone of high land
above the flashing downward race of the Fleet.

This is the Cathedral of the translucent foundations,
the eight silver doors and rafters of sunlight,
the Alchemical House of the First Breath of Creation.

In the multicoloured shadows of this perfect structure   40
I found the people of the golden skin bathing
where eight-sided medicine wheels turn through green foam.

Here in a vision I saw the man-angel water-snake
dipping his head and tail in a font of sunlight,
safeguarding the Cathedral with his magnificent wingspan.

Here I stayed bathing in the sunlight myself
until my understanding went beneath the surface
and I was shown the plan of the song Vale Royal:

A song to throw light on the great secret of London,   50
and the Stance of the Child in the Tree of Life,
the Royal Winged Son of the Liberation;

A song to explain the Golden Quatrain
and the mystical geography of Kings Cross,
a song for all navigators of the night-sea crossing.

Come. A direction into zones of darkness,
a passage to the spaces of discovery begins.
We shall make a voyage to the deep place called Vale Royal.

The mirror and crescent of a jet-black night
now crosses the unclouded zenith of understanding.
We shall study maps of parallel worlds.

A silver ray flashes in the sky of mind.
A spiral train of thought turns backwards.
We burn the lamp of memory to retrace,

To penetrate and know the darkness of time.
Ghostly travellers move in shafts of light,
hallucinated exactly on dead horizons.

We illuminate an existence of other centuries.
We experience the outbreak of metaphysical wars
between the Sunchild and the Spirit of Typhon.

Look. An old man is wandering at night
beside a river, through ruins of Troynovant. See.
There is a child the old man tries to destroy.

It is dark down here. The light is bad.
It is London in the olden days. Take care.
But nothing here is real without belief.

The swan has been waiting all day for the sound of thunder. 310
Sweet flag and willow on the arid bank
are impatient for the waters of the Fleet to rise.

A summer storm has broken over London. Eastward
rain drives over the counting-houses of the Minories
and soaks into the rookeries of Saffron Hill.

The Archflamen and the child of seven take shelter.
Above them the weather-beaten Norman tower
is ready for the winds of seventeen sixty-four.

In the prime of life, with seven hundred years behind,
there is experience in these rain-scarred stones, each block 320
a living cell responsible to the whole edifice.

There is strength and flexibility from rafters to foundations.
The wind plunges over from the Islington ridge,
scooping the old man's words from the doorway,

Flying them, syllables missing, over the night.
They blow away into the fields round Pancras-side.
Is the little boy lost in a trance of the old man's kindling,

Driven to the City of Willows by one whirling hand,
sent where the golden blade lays down the grain,
the human seed which grows on the great earth-plane. 330

The dragon-roads drive through the Royal Vale.
Magnetic mysteries of straight-track and green-lane flicker.
The soul of a child of seven can find these highways!

And this child has seen a tree full of angels. He is different.
How quickly his dark eyes have disappeared upwards!
(Something whispers in the back of the old man's brain.)

The act will raise his standing in the Star-Court of Memphis.
He will read the Book of the Seven High Places.
And the child of the London Madonna in the underworld

Will guard the Temple-Gate out here in the brickfields   340
and dust-heaps of the city, which reach out their hand
and threaten the ancient sites with smoke and extinction!

Rain angles in from the south, bending reeds on the mudflat.
Five blind cygnets exchanging a concave matrix
for realms of unlimited flight see a white explosion.

They see the verge of a different kingdom.
Tonight a new aeon begins in the darkness.
The child speaks against thunder. Listen.

O, there were tall people with bodies like rainbows   350
moving in the fields the other day, walking
among the haymakers near Willan's Farm.

He saw them moving on a road of sunlight,
circles of blue and red fire spinning in their bodies.
In his London accent he talks about his angels.

The eyes of the old man glitter as the boy pipes on;
and a blue javelin of electricity
is hurled through a battlefield of clouds.

Is it the sunchild of Britain's blood-royal?
A black sky rumbles from horizon to horizon.   360
The high winds collide in the wake of the lightning

And the heavens split open again as thunder rolls back.
But the old man hears only the racing drum of his pulse
and the voice which tells him to cut down the lamb in the shadows,

To use the sharp stone which is loose in the western wall,
and tear the body to shreds, and send it down the Fleet,
now in the height of the storm when the blood is hot.

It will save the great earthworks beside the river-bend.
It will save the old tower of Constantine the Great.
The ancient walls of the British Kings will stand,   370

And the Great Star Temple of the Royal Solar Child
will rise as the Red Lodge over the Water.
This is now promised and sealed in flames.

A foul wind from underground howls in the flesh.
It is a bad dream and a long madness.
A storm blows through the hidden City of Willows.

———⇒●⇐———

Seven long years spiral into the stellar void
leaving a hazy blue trail of light
around the blazing axis of the sun. 450

Time races. The unwinding days turn back
and the sunship goes on to the cadence of the second cycle.
But the city reasserts her mundane sublunar position.

Her lost sons and castaways swarm like flies
across the altar of her narcotic fascination.
New-born children see light in the frameways of doors.

London, false to the tower of the first foundation,
whores with her great sons of commerce, groans for brass coinage,
never dreaming of the miracle of her eight directions.

And now, in this late September and anti-climax, 460
our players, who are only shadows,
are moving in their cycles and their seasons.

The wide-eyed child-dancer in the moonlight,
the sunchild and future phoenix of revelation,
stands at his first noon of fourteen under triangles of fire.

He lives with inner voices on Golden Square.
He flies in his night-body over Primrose Hill.
But the Lodge-Pendragon lies in the traitor's place,

A dead man under the midnight quadrant,
a great distance from the physical cities,   470
far from the lesser sunlight.

And now the second solar hero
leaps over the horizon of the song Vale Royal.
He is the youngblood rebel Son of David

Who died in the roofs of the poor Holborn houses
and was buried at the crossroads of the suicide. Selah.
(O King live forever in the city above the city.)

Down here, though his name is on everyone's lips,
and Londoners buy a cheap pocket-handkerchief
stamped with a fair impression of his final eyrie   480

All down the autumn street-markets, still
no-one can decipher his mysterious existence
or translate the magical language of his life.

Let us look around this wilderness of buildings
before returning to his western birthplace
from where we shall track his early-setting star.

Because of a dead child's body rotting on a trash-heap,
and a hard destination, a too-young exit to death,
he is the holy child-martyr of this time.

———⟫◆⟪———

Eleven years old. Thomas the Rhymer.
He carries the sun and moon in his hands.
He stands in the sacred hill of himself.

Three years vanish. He follows the clouds
up through the high summer of his lightning span,
Phaeton in the sky-roads, headlong rider.

Escaping from grey maxims of life below,
he drives hard with the horses of the sun:
his attic the chariot, his lash the hand of fate.

In his dream-body travelling   670
through kingdoms of medieval England,
he lives through the Wars of the Roses in a trance-state.

He casts his eye over neighbouring decades.
The Hundred Years' War. The Lay of the Black Prince. Look!
There are seven epic poems in a dead language.

From the dark core of another life,
in the tongue of a distant time, he ignites
in sixty thousand ancient lines. Selah.

An eight-spoked wheel and a winged sphere,
he is the legend of transmigrations returning,   680
his destiny at first misunderstood.

⟹⟩●⟨⟸

It is late July. The sun, like a red crab,
moves down the hot band of the five o'clock sky.
On the housetops he contemplates his brilliant decline.

The city is dead. Lord X has done his work.
All levelling editors rot on the King's Bench now.
They rave on fire with jail-fever in the Fleet Prison.

The clampdown is tighter than the waistband of Doctor Johnson.
He can find no place for fourteen lines, a farewell   1211
to the dead of the Bengal famine, and he goes hungry.

But after sundown, with his solitary craft
touching the night-wind, the stars, in the act of creation,
he dreams by the ledge with soft nocturnal street-noise.

And when the drone of wheels on Saffron Hill
grows faint after midnight he takes the river-road
northwards through Farringdon to old Battle Bridge.

Here is a pathway lit by the summer moon.
Deep in the silver graveyard of Vale Royal   1220
the dead hours turn towards the dawn,

And the hateful daytime hostilities of the town.
He has traced so many useless circles
through the smoking labyrinth of London. Look.

The moon sinks towards America on her orbit.
He is weighing his chances in the coming winter,
an untouchable poet with the press-laws at his back.

Should he now walk the dusty road down to Bristol
and face the sneers of those who had known
he was nothing all along, a wind veering nowhere?   1230

He admits that his moon is in the house of imprisonment.
But free-will cannot hang fire for any planet.
He questions the priority of the stars.

He will break their wheels of predestination
that turn below the horizons of life,
eclipse their action with his latest work.

In the winged language of his African poems,
with fantastic mosaics and regions of transmography,
he is setting in motion the cycles of legendary London.

Obscure recollections; a world passed out of mind:
he sings the mystery of the Sanctum Regnum.
He knows the country under Angel Ridge. 1240

Where a green king sways overshadowing the incline
on the broad side of Primrose Hill, at Shakespeare's Oak,
the door of midsummer stands open to hidden lands.

Where Parliament Hill, green athanor,
lies circled with lakes of solar light,
the island of free-speech rises from the first matter.

The subterranean aspects of Pentonville involve
the alchemical hill-chamber and underground watchtower
of Merlin, a deep laboratory of Grail-science, 1250

A furnace fired with the daylight tracking of stars,
a megalithic rectilinear construct of great stones
laid down underneath Islington before the Flood.

The Tower was raised on the White Mound of London
with a red mortar in the traditions of darkness.
The ravens are souls of men who rode on the wheels.

Underneath the latter-day cranium of King Lud,
the modern dome of a questionable enlightenment,
a star-temple of the great stone era stands. 1260

Tot Hill, down on the river-bend, also
belongs to the theoretical city of Troynovant.
The voice of the English people bellows

From the swamps of Westminster, sunk in the wide reach.
(Here is Thorn Island, terrible place of the dead,
a great place of power for the Benedictine Order).

And the seventh threshold is in Golden Square,
the seventh cradle of the sunchild, Golden Square,
another winged disc on the serpent perimeter of Zion.

These are seven gates into the urban furnace. 1270
From a rain-scarred tomb towards Marylebone
he watches a last-quarter moon sinking west,

A pale ship foundering slowly on a shore of bricks.
(The slaves look up from their labour in the mausoleum,
burying the royal dust of the House of Troy).

The Sons of the Widow have surrounded Vale Royal
with watchtowers and barbicans to interminate ruin.
They say they have locked the sunchild out of the city.

But the Sons of the Craft forget the eighth gate,
the highway of mercury the messianic Sun-King
rides to the city of the summerland from his zodiac.

He moves in a green lane from Pan's Hill inward,
a white rider with a helmet of gold. Look closely!
The astral dead on this royal solar path

Leave the spectacle of their penalty in Tyburn,
the hanging-tree and the dust which scatters light,
and follow the white rider into Zion,

Glorious pedestrians on pavements of light,
moving through plantations of amarynth, gates of rare metal,
into the terrestrial heaven of the Garden of the Sun.

But the Sons of Chrome know nothing of the eighth gate.
(If you look into the calendar of a man of pleasure
you see no days encircled with gold.)

The moon is gone. He leaps from the tomb,
and turns in darkness beside the Fleet River,
waiting for the clouds to catch fire on the ridge of Islington.

1280

1290

Thomas the Rhymer. He shadows an old tramp
moving up the Gray's Inn Road, a stumbling derelict,
bloody from the gin-dives, inching along in sunshine,

A friendly soul on the road to taste the good waters
from the brass cups on chains at the Well of Saint Chad.
He prophesies drinking himself into second childhood.

He swears by Saint Chad, the patron-saint of new creatures.
He lumbers northwards, old boots grinning at the front.
But is he a man or the spirit of the shape-shifter Merlin?

Thomas, Thomas. He believes too much.   1450
He has drunk too deeply from the River of Wells.
He is mad by every measure of a standard man.

—————➤●◄—————

A traffic of clouds moves in long trains
down the nocturnal avenues of the sky.
He stands on the ancient earthworks, self-complete.

He has seen the hidden city of fusion
where dream and action merge their qualities
under flags of the microcosmic heaven.   2010

Now he is facing the day of hard work.
He bathes his face and drinks from the River of Wells.
(O the waters of life from the fast-streaming Fleet.)

The moon wears a mask of his face in the river.
He leans too far on Battle Bridge, moonstruck,
and laughs, Thomas of Britain, axis-man.

In the pale relief of a daybreak landscape he turns,
moving through an endless graveyard of medieval times,
starting for modern-day Holborn, still in his dreams.

(A strange light shines in the River-Valley of the Treasure-House.
Look! The southern ships of Augustine are sailing.
The altar-stone floats on the Fleet's silver road).

But here, just here, under white ground-mist,
a black door yawns in the earth, wide open,
the subterranean house of rotten walls.

He watches the ridge for the Waterbearer rising,
and crosses the void of no foundation. One step,
and he falls outstretched into darkness, plunging many nights.

2021

———⟫●⟪———

Here is a meadowland with a swift river.
The lambs roll in the warm grass
and the water sparkles by blue reeds.

Here is a hill, a high cone of land by the river.   2260
On the hill is the church with the walls of white water
and the rafters of golden sunlight.

The doors are wide open, the eight doors of silver.
The choirs come up on the winding road from the river.
They sing the excellent song of charity.

The golden wind that made the sunlight
blows through the open doors. Everyone can see it.
The people love this temple as they would their own child.

They bathe from the banks of the beautiful river,
under the flags and jewels of the eight-spoked wheels.   2270
The garlands of trigrams glisten.

Long after the catastrophes of fire and ice,
the ship of mirrors with the summer stars
foaming under her keel returns,

Rounding the promontory of Bolerium.
Merlin looks down at the triangle of her wake
and reads her origins in the waters of the sun.

She is coming from the very-far-distant islands,
coming from the harbours of Avalon.
The sunchild dances in her seven masts; 2280

Her rainbow-wake is a serpent beneath him.
With Egyptian figureheads and crystalline decks,
she sails in the delta of the flowing-through-the-fixed.

The dolphins turn cartwheels in the mirrored stars and moons
as they guide this ship to the temple docks,
under the cone of light on the sacred river.

Beams flash out from her crystal cargo
as she sails between the oak and willow,
between the translucent water-palaces.

The people bathe in the hot African rains. 2290
The wind dries the golden sunlight on their skin.
They bathe in the green wells that rise up foaming.

To dare the incarnation; to take the road in silence.
To know the ascension; to will the resurrection.
The song shimmers in the golden people.

The moonboat anchors and folds her silver sails.
The sunchild dances in the golden masthead.
The Royal Winged Son has made the Great Return.

He was born in the secret beginning of the universe,
in the alpha and maytime of the stars,   2300
and returns through an endless chain of islands

To the country floating over all horizons,
to the headlands of the highest world
and the City of the Golden Canals.

from *India Cantos*

Canto I

On wild horses from the city of sky-blue pillars,
main pylons of the Alexandrian shadow,
over the massif centrale of gunslinging Afghanistan
cosmic rays bombarded high Mazari passes
preparing you somewhat for the flatlands ahead
where infant parrots cried the names of the dead
in blue-green flocks. And there you bribed a fat Saint Peter
to release you with clearance-papers through the Khyber Pass
to the cool hotel-rooms of heaven and Lahore.

And within the shadow of doubt, alone in India,
everything silhouetted scarcely against this continent,
arcane vastness of night, black mother of extremes.
And somewhere behind the Golden Temple complex
more preconceptions were violently laid to rest,
and gradually you left the city like twilight,
remembering the huge angelic doorman of the country,
giant sword-bearer on a smoke-blue platform,
grand mythological welcome extended to everyone,
adolescent overland road-travelling lone-wolves, free spirits;
also the golden ship anchored in a white dream-harbour
full of the chanting of her god-intoxicated crew;

you, stepping barefoot across warm flooded marble
hearing the tap of drum-shaped India, far from London.

But then along with the legendary eighty-eight thousand
you took the narrow road north to everlasting life.
The south was full of death. You were not to know yet.
Bodies on ice. Frenchmen with no papers. Lotus-eaters.
But liquid gold and underwater horses carried you,
playacting the part of a pilgrim all over again,
with holiness beneath the dignity of civilization.
And you of the wanderlust went up through the foothills,
not really aware that you heard someone calling.

O deep burning presence, O dreadlocked godman,
ash-smeared lord of the cosmos living hand to mouth,
clownlike saint whose way crossed mine in the mountains
when all figureheads down on the earth were in flames,
O true silversmith of the straight gaze and steady position,
look out from the past through my page to the flickering eyes
travelling these white landscapes from left to right,
hold them steadily as you held me in the anchorhold,
I, beyond the reach of guiding-forces as I travelled
eastward, away from the empty sky of the west.

A man in his time unstamped by the trademark of years,
a man of trajectories out of the world, and yet

he had advanced in the bureaucratic graveyard of railways
far to the south with the noonday shunting of corruption
all round the branch-lines and little feeders. Government servant,
like others expected to wink at clockwork blunderings,
regular carnage of a single-track game of chance,
he would not, took exit on principle, changed the points,
derailed a career, obstinate proud heart bleeding.
So much for the bad farce of going anywhere in life!
Wife and children vanished into the Brahminic establishment.
She went like ruling-class Shakti back to her palace,
leaving the madman with seed in outstretched hand
burning in the midday asylum of black heat, glazed,
strange husbandman in the sacred agriculture of darkness.

You meanwhile, disenchanted tenant of the pinewoods,
stupefied yourself by monstrous infallible masters,
doctrinaire hypnosis of usual predatory disciples,
you, on your late-evening sleepyhead trackway home,
ran into salvation with the sweet laughing face,
with the old dismantled chromium umbrella
cradled in the lap, imaginary ritual instrument
whose music was heard in a musicality of laughter.

Mahatma, who called the thunder and lightning
out of the deep blue Himalayan skyways,
you took the candidate back to your tumbledown
shack with no doors and no windows, abject cabin
halfway up the far side of somebody else's hill.
And what did you teach there? Out of a legend-wheel turning
the pitch-black tantric philosophy of the rose,
forbidden marriage of joy with ascetic perfection,
flesh no longer a dictatorship of rotteness when the tantras
significate the merely sexual with secret meaning?
Yes. And you were questioned with blood-red urgency
about this high-speed romantic night-train to paradise.
But sometimes, joking apart, you would speak of the punishment
where hot locomotives in the dense smoke of traction
carry many unclean down to the collisions of death
while family men in sunlight make adequate excuses
as a wreckage of duality burns in the junction. Warning,
as a man you showed me the fault in your own mortality,
told of the girl-child who meddled with your fiery vessels,
little one who channeled out the skin from her left cheek with acids
so that you worked twenty nights in deep hell without sleeping
to remake her half-ruined face by the royal art. Yes!
Then with sunflare explosions of intensity you spoke,
illusion by great solemn lights and detachments surely,
O long-haired one removed from the earth in general,

coming from a long distant line of Deccan saints, you
with your thin brown frame sustaining all poisonous alkaloids,
wind-clad master of the high ground and pine-decked mountains,
lord of the snow-line, old acquaintance of wild animals,
godman for whom the sky-women came down at night.
But tortures eating your heart out made you seem human,
the superman who could still put his forehead in the dust
to pray for the dear ones of his household as well as for his powers,
the children of his marriage-bed as for miraculous virtues.

And so Mahatma in the early days of our discourse
you and I went through the pinewoods talking and laughing
to bundle dry wood for your sacred fire of oblations.
And having the light work in order we sat down to rest.
And resting once in the noon-fire hours I returned
the round way of time, going back as you asked me, remembering.

I was a child of the great London fogs. Once again
I walked hand in hand with my Dickensian grandfather
through little Pottery Lane of the yellow atmospheres
where morning fogs gathered from the huge bomb-craters
where they slept in the hollowed-out ground behind my house.
Perhaps some shard of clay from the pottery workings
attracted my wise old friend to the problem of breakage.

And very gently then, having me firmly by the hand,
he touched the unspeakable subject of death. And I
cried out in my half-understanding of the mystery,
the fog making all forms ghostly and intangible
and only my grandfather's hand to hold onto
and he gently speaking of the great separation.

Excruciating pleasure-wheel, life goes on and on,
low-points and topside days succeeding. Grandfather,
old mountaineering poet under Mercury had not long
before big landsliding mortality took him, and I
stood with one hand extended in the direction of memory.
But announcement of the shadow alerted a five-year-old mind.
And before I crossed over to the transatlantic paradise
grandfather knew of a poem, the Comedy of London,
a poet of milk-teeth tried to pronounce in his heart,
song of a cabin-boy sunchild who came home laughing
after the great island-wars and dying in the west.

And one other time this dumbfounded grandson
spoke to his wise old friend about the destroyer.
And this was after a damned young existence was saved
by one already dead and lengthwise in a coffin. I remember
Victorian houses flashing backward in twilight
as I stood up on the pedals to take on the impossible,

accelerating down the forbidden pavement of November
to find no braking-power in my hand to hold back
the death-ride into a busy crossroads of the city
where I became a small burnt-offering on asphalt,
laid on the smoking skid-marks of a great London bus,
almost, except for demons in tall black headgear
proceeding across my way in slow-motion! I saw them
walking the uncanny interrupted death-gait alongside
a black limousine of Orpheus in low-gear cruising,
a black graveyard-train on its way down to Hades. Dear God!
The walking dead saw me coming in the fogs and scattered,

apocalypse of undertakers running without dignity
as I thundered down on my child-sized wild horse
to ram the black Rolls with a broadside of bicycle,
funeral-car of priceless bodywork, to somersault
headfirst by the handlebars into that mobile flowerbed.
And I remember then, all true, amid the shouting of mutes,
someone with a hat like a sky-scraping factory chimney,
the most satanic gentleman in black, towering in rage,
reaching down for me, spreadeagled out in the flowers,
hauling a bloodstained and catatonic passenger
out of the coffin-bearing sunship from the underworld,
shaking and cascading rose-petals to the pavement,
to stand me up, boy, on a penumbrous landing-stage

to listen to the self-important bellowings of pall-bearers,
scandalized lamentations of sackcloth and ashes,
confusion on the part of the badly-paid servants of death.

O grandfather Ashley, Blampish as I called you, wise old man,
only you heard this confession, how my life was extricated
by a dead man lying on a splendid mattress of flowers,
who shared that paradise-bed for a scallywag's landing,
who afterwards always in cycling dreams of recurrence
seemed to be peering up through up through a rose-petalled glass
winking one eye at the small London tearaway, smiling.

jennifer chalmers

Peat

> Ye've had a cruel mither, Willie
> ....
> But we shall sleep in Clyde's waters
> Like sister and like brither.
>
> *Clyde's Waters*

Aloof slaves pack for
another, her mind for
anyone, for the clouds.
The moor continues, lie
down loving me.

And play to conceal it.
Where are the old mounds
now? Sorrow cannot leave
an explanation, as loss
leads up to my house

An ancient tale, a moth
around temptation, the language
riots then expires or goes
wandering across these hollows
searching for the border

fir fear fields floor
blowing out brown blaze

white wet wall witches
clothe clear circle
plaid peace

divided
ledge
glow gibberish gentle
unchained uncontrollable
savage sinister snow

trembled
rarely rage
ashes
violent
hurt

So smother me bodily
fold me with hope
and when I can't see
a plank of a roof
make me a couch of oak

or wipe it with a wet cloth
cross the old white
floor, find a look out
over the fields. Then turn
to tend the blaze with appalling

skill. The candle round
this writing
I blow it out.
Listening, willing this blue
before the moment parts

subtler rays, passing, fix
the heart, as my favourite wool
lies listless and remote.
Words turn to pose
dreaming of a part

to tag the infinite
as slowly, a passionate curve
a little fear, fermenting
triggers depression. A delicate
drifting, the desire

enclosed in the night.
Desolation
might leave, let
say, a oneness
dance there with our shadows
caressing, snaring

your mouth
your lonely glow
restlessly washed

with rain, to spring
dark evenings

looking at each other.
The moors outside
the flock disturbed.
Lovers, pure mirrors
masochistic, a landfall

A mystic gate, heart stained
melancholy moves, fanatical
Hope synthesised, the miracle
to disappear
as a syllable

difficult to know.
I had a warm
pinkness, a cold papa
and now embrace, infernally
goblins in the sentence

Yet the landscape becomes soft
lying in shadow. Burnished
fragments of history carefully
reappear. She is here
Her face is pale. She has
that lonely tarnished glow

as the evening light grows
lavish there lands
a knock out blow. It's a sign
for chanting.

Those two bloody sticks

these tattered clothes
the scent of travelling
stones, going tranquilly
out of one's depth, with
fatal grief as sail

to some invisible extinction.
A lovers' perfect leap meets
an obscure silence, heaven
on a bleak journey, a walk
desolate and austere; here with

violent fears and fearful
rage, I am lonely
to the last possible loss
smiling as the fire illuminates
the striking hands.
There's blood
on the surface. Tensions
ripen in a real messy kitchen.

Eat   Eat
hand to hand the flow of

sidelined quips
pearls lies notches strips
to fail with you, not
an angel, your rational sadness
irresistibly spread

scattered like bird seed
as we wander out, back along the path
to exchange our pleasures, origins
the range of mountains, the endless
riddle within. This restless

dramatizing, ferocious release
so hectic sensual, the darkening
dream tempestuous and icy
makes almost normal
nostalgia, enables

death to flower. I
stick some tulips in, vocal again
and my breath 'smells earthy strong'.

andrew brewerton

Sirius

— 'kin ell ar mon, what yow fookin wânt nah then?

— Four's split. We're doin number four.

— Yow cor de that! Fower! Six is cracked an all ay it? We'm all set nah!

— So I'm changin it. For fuck's sake Tricksey, y've bin workin four all day. It's wide open, y' bloody know it is.

— 'kin jaysus!

— Okay so what yer mekkin Monday wi' no bleedin metal ay? Daywork is it? Come on let's shift the siege for chrissake.

— Awroit! Av it your fookin road! Yow'm the fookin gaffer eh lads? 'kin arsoes.

Abruptly we stand off and it's the business again, two figures glazed with sweat and burning a moment at the furnace mouth.

— Doh yow tek n'notice on im, And. Ee ay all there, Tricksay ay.

— 'is all there all right, Col. I know what 'is after.

Piecework over, now everywhere what molten glass remains is scooped all orange-honey in the heavy ladles from each furnace -

crucible. All about it hisses and crizzles in vast wheeled kettles of soon boiling water, the spilt strings and trails of it cooling fast into transparency: ice and fire.

The pressured sounds and weak haphazard rhythms of the work now score the slow expiry of this shift. My breath sinks all sickened with salt tablets, the waste-flavour of a sop to creeping dehydration and struggling productivity. In the overheated element I don't prevent the infringement on each sense of bruising noises, sharps of textured violence. Moving, still you watch your back for burning irons or freak translucent razors. I take it all in regardless. Observation thickening with forms beyond purpose, the pointed remit: *handle* this then.

The siege erected around four, already now the men are picking through intense heat at the furnace clay wall. The fired scales of it fallen they rake clear, and gradual debris rings the scene.

We frayed and enervated each retain this triggered calm from working all the still August day. Their eyes looking white rings blasted beneath green visors. A few battered fans wave ineffectually, circulating the unavoidable temperatures.

The clay skin is stripped and bricks now splinter with the blows of picks and crowbars. The team approach in pairs, they strike and lever, shoot their strength and turn. Eyes closed as though unneeded, they move to known positions speaking rarely as the next two walk forward. Refractory bricks shatter. The great fender blocks loosen, show their seams and, suddenly, topple.

At this the rusted sheet curtain is lowered, shielding tremendous heat, and we break off to air our forearms out of gauntlets, turn the salt-creases of our eyes away and wipe sweat. Salt, salary. I linger by the furnace, in a few seconds drying the shirt that's soaking cold again upon my back. And listen.

Now the clinking choreography of glassmaking and inherent roar of gloryholes has given over to this furnace swell and high insistence of a few cicadas living in the warm dirt of an accidental climate. I listen rooted, kindly, the furnace resonance claiming soon vacated limbs.

— Ee thinks is off wum a-fookin is missis, an' ee ay nowhere fookin finished wairk yit!

I focus quickly and wincing grin the feint con of acknowledgement into stale and sweatsore his face. Les. Yes, back now the fender rubble is glowing, pushed aside. They brush the way clear to wheel in two handled ploughshafts on fixed axles, a lever ram and the iron chariot with its set pincer arms for gripping ironwise about the pot. As they jerk upward the sheet curtain a sudden front of heat scalds to swallow, has you gasping. The pot sticks and shines amazingly as they work the lever, jabbing long irons into the light.

Slowly it unsettles and we tease it from the glazing ledge, prise it clear. Moving swiftly to avoid the glare as now it eases fully out, not scraping the crown arch. Another wave as the gas flame exposes in the furnace heart, the slow white shadow dance of its atmosphere. Then the rust curtain they drop swaying and with mechanical theatre.

Pot secure now in its chariot, the intense blaze sears and darkens all other view.   An egg incandescent in its ant jaws. Phoebus in his fiery course. The burnt day blackened in a kind of sunrise.

Day Break

Some thorn of her tiled sleep spun
         lovely   slow to fear
dislodging as slate litter the first hours
         insist   we wake under
the familiar roof to silence   her
         long attention   half in league

from far a lone car rousing   breaks
         as a wave of the former turnpike
wakens   and another   you are
         the breakers   the early coal
road ribboned with calamity burning
         in the generations of fuel

the links of stone loosen to her
         mute favour   a dream recessive
in the yellow rent of the sky
         over Coventry   day's precarious
tenure   a house at the surface   riven
         in the lives of the colours

the voyage back floods these reefs before
       with golden hindsight
seams awash openly now   a loose thread
       draws the landscape in
       to nearer coastal glamour   *a fair child*
sleeps behind the thorny hedge

of the pages which follow   the waves
       no more than traffic outside
roof intact   you do not wake her
       hawthorn ruched and woven
above the curtain light implies
       a quiet landfall   like a detonation.

john cayley

island 01

mountain beautiful limbs spread
eagled under seagulls circling spring
rises islanded *bare* island beside to lie

ocean the broad irises upon this if I
circling *island* broad filling and hale
and temples beautiful furnished
lammas morning from top beside
bright *flesh* on the broad filling

oileán 01

sléibhe lá breá *oileán is* thógfainn suas

fola *ea* thógfainn *do chorp* fhéin

lúnasa bheirfin is deoch slánaithe do

fiondruine gan dom bogóideacha

threabhfainn mara amháin

droimeann bhraillín gléigeal iad

t'fhabhraí thabharfaidís gléigeal

scuabacha nuair uirthi *i* thiocfainn

from: *Songs of my Heart*

VII

When I was young and foolish —
following strings, drifting on song —
I roamed the West End, and danced
With mistresses, madams and maidens.

There seemed no end to sensual delight
Until broad daylight saw me stumble in the street.
Thousands spent, but then no glint of gold,
Before it's gone, it always seems enough.

Tug the reins, turn the horse's head
for home, behind me, far in my longing.
I'd set out for warmer weather heading north.
What's the use, now I know I'm lost?

after Ruan Ji (210-63)

Of Time

Whose heart is marked with his intention
     resents the shortness of the day,
But those whose years are withered by sadness
     know the length of the night:

Pull 'round a cloak. Walk in the open court.
Look up to see south-faring wings — the geese in flight.
Dark Shadow follows the shapes around,
While floating sounds return where you no longer sit.
Why should the light breeze swirl and shudder
When the new moon rises on your right,
And from crowds of stars held up
In jet, the zodiacal band spreads out?
Cicadas sing in the tall trees,
In the barn on your left the owls hoot.
Wisps of cloud are tangled in dark hair,
The dew descends, your cloak is wet.

When life was good, its shadow did not pause,
The stars which rose, before you realized, set.
The fear of winter's swift approach was certainty,
As frost catches up the breath and binds it tight.

Leaves fall, after the wind's push,
Cut from the tree, they join the flowing light
     of time.

after Fu Xuan (217-78)

tertia longmire

from *The Table Leaks its Object*
transcriptions from graffiti found on thirty school examination
desks abandoned in south London during 1996

Marcus got a fit ass Adrian from 9T past the
science exam I hope ha ha ha I hate exams How
old was Hitler when he died? As old as your mum
Ha Ha I love you more today than yesterday
Warriors Hunter E E in 9L did his geography exam
The one I love is S....dy Nini for Nini for ever till
death do us part. (Amen) in Jesus name Stockwell
Park School M.Y. is a playboy Fun Otis Elavators
LCC did his history exam What does the condom
say to the dick Fulham are the best Whoever sits
here there mum's jokes. I woz ere Yes Brother
Michael Harrison 94 Then I left the shit school
called Stockwell Park School. Hyper 93 Sir Funkalot
in his Portugese exam I am bored to death because
I have finished my exam in half time is gay Why is it
people never pass exams Good Luck it was a bit
hard I was not here because I was fucking your
mum Catia loves Victor Hit Man Lisa managed to
fail. Charlotte 1964.

I love Mames but not for long. Miss Culture Sister Handy Mr Donaldson woz ere and call on all Ballboy Student Supporters to help fulfil his desires Boy Kelvin was here codename Alice 'Nirvana' rule 95 Sister Dredge is your M. C. Sugar. Krazy Kids Krew. Ruff Nicola Sey So. your pussy clothing. SAM HAVE BEN TAKE AN EXAM FOR THE SECOND TIME IN MONDAY 17INE JUNE 1991. 5see 8oxb need nirvana succeeded Caroline Perez is a Lezbian Go on read the table Boris Beker woz ere for an electronic exam 88 Stew Pot was here Jam Rock versus Stone Love Delroy woz ere doing biology Daddy Bear Jewelry ran health crops learn Black Brown Red Orange Yellow Green Blue Purple Grey White Give me food food Sugar Levi an de opar Sister Jay de Bubblers Miss Culture de me power Sister Dredge cool and Deadly Sister Andy she Lyrics well Randy. Mad Chopper Big Shot For a good time dial 999 Mim Rahella Rani Marco Wren Yes MY Name Is Babbling Drab And Me Is A Big Sape geography exam was a piece of piss penis MY PEN IS Snoot Rules nicely and Samantha 10T Bitch I LOVE NAMES Boo Cora was in maths mock exam I love you Grobelar Neal Hansen Lee Dalglish Mark Johnstone Horse Radish Hard Boiled Eggs. I love Caroline but she don't love me Kalvin was ere ginger kid Lodge is don.

Roddy Framed Chris Tata Fiona Michael Vicky Sticky Regents Posse Cool Rasta Spurs are questionable D. Brown died here over worked in English Scent The Bluebells filthy Ruth but J. Fern is a dad The Playboy Posse are Danny Peter Otis Neil and Guy Nemso Nemsa Nerriso Nerissa Elton John I Love You Helen Cowan suffered her G.C.E. chemistry theory. I shit myself here SEXPRESSION Elton John I think you're great I really do love you You're such a hunk I love your style I'm glad you love me too by his lover George X X X Elton John will help me through this exam. What the fuck mate silly sod you mother fucker traitor you bastard you cunt John's girl is pregnant Ninja was definitely here Bengali Bastards too much incence insense Ninja you can't Wing Chi Tai Chi Twa Kwandu Kendo. I shot J R Corey Hemmings Prophet Posse

GET IT STACEY FOR MARTIN Iwant your pussy STACEY LOVES MARTIN suck pussy hole GANG BANG STACEY wants to fuck Martin Ashes to ashes dust to dust if it wasn't for pussy your dick would be puss. It was easy I was ear exam geog. and I love Anthony BAD RUDE GIRL Richards mum came to my house one day. When my mum sent me to make some tea for the old slag she followed me into the kitchen and asked me to suck her thin breast. I said no because Richard was my friend but then she dropped her knickers. Sign the great T. p.s. she is a dirty fat slag Dean and Michael are so bitchy BOUNCE so sad HELLO GOODBYE.

I have put a curse on this table so whoever has his exam on this table has failed. Fuck off about your curse because I'm sure to pass I just failed my electronics exam on 24th of May 1982 Punk mother fuckers I failed this shit and I'm going to be a road sweeper. Michelle was here failing her energy module test for double science. I failed my exams here. F.K. sat here thinking if only I had studied my D 'n' A Little Bog Creep. Sharon Seymour sat here in commerce and cheated Lyn Stowell sat behind her. Harvey sat opposite. Michelle has also failed her biology exams at this table. MASK Mark Jones of 9K took mock. M. Garcia sat here saying fuckin' el what's this. ANGEL Ring 671 0362 for a fucking good time. Simon Tedeschi I will love you always LUV Michelle Ryder Date Reference goods Goods Purchased Company from which goods came Muz sat in front. metabolism I failed my German here die FUED sprachen sie Deutsch wein. elimination like little boys 6 - 100 KALOUSE CHANTELLE Good Luck I am Leaving after 5 long years at this school 72 - 77 I've just done my last exam HA HA. I HOPE ALL YOU BASTARDS FAIL - LIFE BELT - Florence MC child practice 1977 I don't know the answer to my exam that's why I'm writing this shit Good Luck Big Head distance pressure work resistence mass volume force volts hope.

Yeah you would you old slag wogs meat Food and Nutrition the worm that turned whoever sits here is a wanker, 1664 I like a laugh and a hot warm bath and a whole days sense of humour well if it rains today like it did before I'm gonna have to leave a little bit sooner. Down at the park where you need to be older and you sure don't look like Madonna. Rod Stewart this is rubbish punk rubber Goebbels satisfaction I'm doing well, yesterday I failed English, today I fail maths Can't be bad can I? Juan was here doing his stupid house craft exam which he has not passed this exam was fucking hard so was mine Peace from Cheeks emotional WOMACK AND WOMACK Nayivor done her Food and Nutrition THE SAM EVERLY COOKEY BROTHERS BUDDY JIM WROTE THIS BECAUSE HE FELT PISSED OFF WHEN HE FUCKED UP HIS PHYSICS EXAM joy the jam Lavern did well Good Lick young male would like to meet girl with a tight one AFC kick arse by Games plus Elsa Cherry and Vicky woz ere sitting maths CSE / O level 1986 and we think we failed (joke) ha ha A. Smith is a slag who likes men with big balls useless load of crap my stupid computer studies sex pistol Did I sweat for my building construction you bet by Mark Alan of Spurs a grave situation Circuit 1 shit face Helen sat here for her Aora Jerry Jamison Funking Hard especially whoever sits here will fail their exam who died as soon as it was handed in I love women and wogs love Pauline Please do not park here space in constant use God save England Join the race The Jewish House the dying zone anorak history is made.

225

Mark White thiefs Nicholas was not here ha ha ha "YES I"! ebony posse inna de area murder murder dis an de ebony posse Johnathan Cook failed again BLEAH failing chemistry John O'Rourke did not pass his Human Biology so I don't give the fuck King Tubby Saxon Deh Bout FUCK IN HELL your mum Barbara sat office practice here I love me cause no one else will Barbara Funk Ebony Posse rule de area under Roots and Culture.

Baby Dragon Man Utd. F.C. RULE Diana 7w 1996 Foxy Trigger woz ere someone said that Linton is fit (not) my your venom VENOM FIX Kinhead soldier BOY sgt. ANDY Stephanie loves ANDY I fucked up in my exam. When I need fucking help do I get the fucking help no I fucking don't SPIKEY Left wishes you luck love my Aston Chelsea rule O.K. I failed maths before even starting thoroughly Charlene 1994 If you read this your Dad so do your exam or else Sty & Vicky wos ere doing technology exam. If you read this it's your mum so get on with your exam or else. Good Luck. Helen failed mock CSE chemistry here 6-12-82 Fuck all Man These Exams Are Fucking Cramp Fuck All aspect Fuck Off You Kill all Bangos and Arsenal not I set hire ond post me spilling exiame 2.9.94 NIPPER Good Luck whoever sits here. Thanks. Teachers make me sick and me and me too hear hear and me and me me too also me and me and me Help I failed geography in 1978 Stef 9K done her Technology exam here The Clash Shakes Rampa Ratty Stallion Cat Eyes Ninja Scoobie Hyper I want my mummy Help Life Sucks I hate Why cant I do this exam Profit Promote Place Producer Precinct Stockwell Manor Lives I'm a bobyguard Stockwell Park now love. Von Chu nearly O.K. THE VEGY changing job Don Dada Woz Ere 93 abcdefghijklmnopqrs HFC SUCKS whoever reads this is a tramp Write this you are don't be a pussy all your life I'm in love and I love the feeling Ferooza (curry) loves John Stef woz ere doing Technology exam been and gone. Tony Osborne is cool. I DID COME cacth coch.

Stop reading the table. I was here but now I dissapear. Stacy S. loves Martin S. Rushna 4 Rohim Mohammed has a buckhead Oasis Bitch Beware maths exam is hard English is easy Science is a piece of cake WANKER Robert Miles, tell me a story, a fable. It's fun fun fun for your mum mum mum. River Mersey Mary Your mum has no legs King Elvis Lives. Sumo. HipHop. Bonjour I love names but not long C.W.is gorgeous I wait, wait You wanker I was here but now I have gone I left my name to turn you on. Cummings All male teachers are wankers. Mars Jarge Sound. Shannaz loves Gump Chantelle Junks. Boyzone. MONA Tots T.V. hosipal hospial Shane is my man Ian Wright and Ahmed Nasser Chants was ere doing her home ec. exam DARE DEVIL Skunkihamawe wadada I man Righteous Blood and fire Conquering Lion Yeah up Wattic Bongo Dreadie All Hail Hails Haile Salassie Millwall F.C. TARA CHANTS creator Nirvana

CEM woz ere Stockwell Soul Syndicate They was all ere sitting they're A'level solid soul exam and they passed. Sharon woz ere ere she woz woz she ere yes she woz Kathy woz ere M.C. Hammer came to my school Elaine Brown Funkye woz ere 5.6.85 Shass Donni Massi Angie Di Nikki Soul Patrol Freeki Cheeki D Mystery M Lady Freak Sexy Di Kinky Nikki English Sucks Sociology O'level exam 10.6.85 Miss P.H. A Definate Fail A population increase Unemployment Financial Aid (Social Security) Over Crowding in Houses (children unable to afford their own homes) Birth Control Better Medicines Better Accomodation or Heating Facilities to prevent whooping cough Arsenal R Shit If you notice this notice you would notice it's not worth noticing MASK 4 COLONEL BUCKER Hungie is a vain bastard 15/5/96 Fuck the law smoke a draw TIGER STYLE DIG DOLLARS Michelle woz ere re sitting English Language O' Level 13.11.84 WICKED POSSE Paws Jugalise Killing the Weed Mask Mohamed Ali Suma Keita Timmy Cuitable Cuitablly Dread Jackie Smith Geoff. B. was sitting here at this very desk to do his physics mock exam One Nation take a trip on an e live your life in extasy.

by the year 3000 he will be a rock star signed HIS BIGGEST FAN. Den Dance Energy JAZZ me myself and I was bad say no go 3 feet high and rising Too Rough Hyperactive Kiss his was the best Ninja Kid run tings wicked med fom red heat prepared crazy 4 Sarah If you know what this means you are so fucking clever Bizzy Bone for Georgina are you having the problem of not getting a girlfriend call me Samuel Welly on 720 0978 because I'm having the same. Are you having trouble with your Fallopian tubes ring 498 6245 "HOME AND AWAY" Lazerdrom is Pukka Rude Boi and Gal who like Jungle Big up and Push up you chest Jungle is bad respect Jungle will never die Respect to everyone that loves Jungle. Yung is ugly original gangster is here What you looking wanker Krazy Kids Krew Rule Yardie Massive. Big 'up' you status Stockwell Raver rap are pukka Devious Kenny Ken fuck you frosty. Pukka. The Day Will Come.

Madness voice box trachea ribs lung jane
Constantinople english here I sit I love
crumpet wayne crab electronic red skin
Pan De Control Balls Grove for I taking
biology Why did the chicken cross the road.
To sell her eggs at the Co-op Cheek K.C.
Bunky Tracy H woz ere doing office
practice exam YES YOB Madness here I sit
HELP ME police DAD minder Ricardo Rap
'A' Level Sex Exam 1999 Here lays Adolfo
R.I.P.P.S. after maths exam 1977 glucose
plant get the mother father $y = s - x$ hello
pen who said chemistry was easy wish me
luck I'm going on the dole minder was here
taking people on singer sleepy oh shit I've
pissed myself carry it out shelter subs
bronchiole I think I have failed I'm not
bragging Innovators Extremists Rebels

WHITE HEAD BROTHERS Prodigy Dance Hot Summer of 1995 Liverpool LOVE Heloooooooo This one's for Charlene Hall M.F.C. Budwiser from Faiza Fatality SILK SOUL Eddie and Tony = Beagles Baby Baby Baby why are you so Roses Dose wealth you know me completely T. C. 4 PATMA Skeen Kinhead Menace foriegner foriegner Tracy sat here B - Forever Snapper and Snapper and Troofer Chelsea Rule Agro Not beat it Football Scar I am saying whats up to everyone. You know how we do it . Janet Jackson socked M. Kelly mint condition heard except Calm Brazil Southern oxygen oxegyn oxsigin How to pass your life practice reorganisation to athletes or clubs Anna ~~Blacks~~ WHITES are shitty little wanked up jungle bunnys Morrell is smell Colin Gateson was laid to rest here in metalwork 1975 Trombet laid to rest here in memorial of the house craft I sat here very confused so did eye Amy sociological Falk Off Argentina Bertram Bertwhistle dead mania contento fimberesse de duled da dayte whatever the weather Raja 4 Rani Respect to Almighty Raja Anam and Hifzur are Gaylords 95 fuck this June woz ere January 75 Michael Vidal champion lover Bullfrogs fuck off I love you Fatma from someone you don't know HELP Runtings and Tings No Run Them See (5-7-95) (14K) I got all grade ones last year so who needs exams Keep Falklands British Falklands belong to Argentina fuck off Britain. Peadar leap in a Portugese Exam A joke between your legs I feel free Bad Mother Fucker 1996 Ninja from Tulse Hill GOLD TEETH and bid in a Brixton Sir Coxsone International Fuck Face Liam was here... IS GOING TO GET HIS HEAD KICKED IN BY THE CLASH CITY ROCKERS you're joking my HD was here. The One and Only Eddie laughs Eddie trying things Help me Help me YOU'RE GOING TO FAIL

CROSS ROADS roles IMAGE done English Life is a terrible strife I failed don't worry O.K. Elsa 4 James afforded what is gay by a government piano idea tap stamp stamps drabble Monty passed economics here 2.6.86 Ha Ha GOOD Six Sexy Ladies. Timmy was ere wet I was raped at the age of 8 all my friends think I stink my name is Paul Danton MAZE FM yeah I've been there many times and its BAD AlexIs. I went to Maze too with Alexis she's right it's wicked Cheeky D. Soul Patrol Delisia Sherise Alisha Marianne Wikkiana Diane Fascists are bastards God is dead Lady Di's a bitch Look to what I said 2 gametes for one ova 2 ova for one gamete Stereophonic in the mix 3 Callingham House Clapham Road FLICKS 96 FUNK Later Stockwell Park try not to fucking miss this shithole I HATE SCHOOL you're not the only one. I love school (well maybe not) Kwami 4 Monty 4 Gary 4 RICHARD Wandsworth Wankers Massive Dicks Jungalise I love Michael Jackson I don't I really was stumped on my metalwork mock test and fucking failed syphilis Lady Freak is a proud member of Soul Patrol. The sexiest all girl Soul Syndicate In South London. Shut up. If you would like maths exams answers rlng 0171 733 4502 and ask for Rhodd. You cried with me, you're locked deep inside of me, you found the better side of me, Carry me (Flintlock 1977) mix with water absorb makes a gel gelatine when cooled break up when cooled whats wrong with you man physics is crap you're not wrong mate.

Llewwllyn Pemberton sat here and failed his physics Hussain loves Allah David woz ere 93 doing maths CSE mock exam I love sex so do you me too Tony for Janice good Luck with yours Matta Izzy woz ere 4 Rochelle French exam I know I failed but you can't fucking pass every exam Michael of the crazy crew Simon for Kim I fucked your mum remunicent reminiscent train 2kg Pabe of the lazy crew especial C.T. died here mock German 1974 FK woz ere doing Biology Exams 4 july 84 DO YOUR REVISION Charlie sat english mock Who's going down Geraldine for Frank Simpleton (false) Kemi loves singing Yeh Man 1600 Audrey woz ere doing her physics mock exam paper Clifton for Duncan Smart He got his lips stuck in the exhaust pipe Tina was sitting here sweating too Remember that maths is like sex And Monique Your mum was here scratching her big boobs June 88 John Somers waffled his way through part three Enid woz ere wizzing through a maths exam (I think) I couldn't even touch the bloody paper Yvonne Lady Diana Spencer woz ere 25-6-81 having an RS exam Why is there air? We do not exist we are a figment of the imagination. If we are a figment of the imagination who's imagination is it? Peter Potter woz ere doing his English I failed Remember that Maths is like sex You add the bed takeaway the clothes I love Ismat Here I sit am broken hearted passed my exam and only farted M.R. 1980 Bernice is my good friend Lenny Roberts Loser Ron Haslem Winner my finger my thumb my goodness my bum bastard Katia likes .... Detectlve Hogg Large Every Time I was sitting an art exam one day when my bollocks fell off and rolled away John S is a snob O.K. Susan woz ere sitting biology sex exam next to Nathan 29/6182 done missed out COMMUNICATION and Monique.

DIE Punk shit Hope you fail bitch I blow your brains out shit head Bitch Ouch Bitch Bitch dorset road man Liji sucks Hood Bitch Bitch Mega Rules Dean 1992 Your mum my maths Johnathan Cook Physics 9.12.81. What a bore I'll fail what rubbish this is I think I'll have a kip God I'm bored why don't I just leave now. best singer is Vivien I fuck Tara Flynn and Woudy Sidabe 1000 divided by 50 Sex is like maths. pussy hole It was easy Andrew Wayman was late for biology quick boys watch out Liji's in town grab your bum and run SHIRRINS 1996 I got the biggest nut spunk FUCK SCHOOL Quality Street Mums I Love Linlex loves Sarah in 4P I wanna be her boyfriend quickly because I love her truely Kingswood I love W. Sidabe You suck son of a gun A-BONE Brighton I'm doing Chinese can you ere SHOUT SHADE suck My Tag = Angel = Van Chu How to spell his surname don't know how ANGEL FREE

THE BUSH 18 JONES sat his mock foo studies exam here The E X crazy mother fuck and nut This is R. Teap of 5T Darren B was ere on tuesday taking a fucking shit science test and it is boring too. Stacy Spencer in Food and Nuts Kill Niggers was ere 9T6 Ashes to ashes dust to dust if it wasn't for pussy your dick would rust I was here Babynine Ashes To Ashes dust to dust whisper Mandy Classy Master Cast run tings and tings no run them seen yes Wiggy I was here too I love sex phone and ask for me Life is shit HUM HAI RAJA Bubba People in cars cause accidents Accidents in cars cause people. Life is like a pubic hair on a toilet seat, you soon get pissed off. Sarah in 10S for Byron Free sex 377 4969 Karen Turner for Tom Cruise Renault who is a snob Millie sat here 1972 inceidents incedent inceidence wet weather tornado menace this fucking sociology exam is hard taking language was boring and long and easy should be your foot whisper mash stallion are all bastards sign I meet you at the crossroads Mrs. Arsenal life is shit. Love makes the world go round but LSD makes it spin. Snuggles for Luke (practice one)

Episodal inquiry gets bored quickly. The limits send clues.
Inspire to taker theatre soars. Cutter sends also.
Also miner down in the root. The glass fibre pulls out a
cloaked testimony which moans a classic hoarse sound.
Tight poacher concluding ignition. Shot in the side.
Moon move slides into view. Bouncing frozen as the mender dines.

Ruth guzzles her exam into Richards facing science. Loads held by
testing her bitch. Here, could it cover the history in seconds, moulting
at the reason. She shreads Mohammed's I.O.U.'s kissing the surface
shaking the silver pen.

Her strength sucked from the tiny crystall of mourning standing for the
dream her mum's mum passed over. Bruise pressing, a past-time helped
the ugliness up out from the skinner.

Out there, there pausing, the collie mule deals waisted.

Fuel deepens ant houses.

Wraggling the hoist trips fencing a tiny increase. Vanguard robbing
cocks downward to activate again. Myopic dancer swerves onto the law
it taps, and tapper records the device. It asks why the person remains in
the room carving away the shield, the weld now exposed.

Based on action the pills repute a comic shame. Shawling a cover the
print rubs away. A sick lung giggles. A lamenting house. Imagine that

the fire was started by the drugger. Barn ego hollowed across the beam, as an item trapped delicately inside. The thinking fall. Stark base line below an etched metal scratch, rises weighting the burnt wood beams dazzling against the sun light strip.

Key to skull cut short places the puzzle among crocks of soil embedded in throat cushion. Hazelnuts the size of mugs in plastic bags space the rushes into being as the cut is made. Quickly as the glass slips down to trap the frame, daring to gaze upon the scribble, walks around. Trees finger in skull cup, in hand from the cold border fringing each terror in celebration.

An echo fuses the cram along the narrow. Spoke arches as if to bridge, the kind to look for. Ruth sets to remembering her brighter.

Pressing matter into the cloak she slides across. Tuner picks out the final gauge hitting the deep. An approach is made. Memory fades with its gender into the fluid game.

david amery

Virtual Garden

The flatness is
deceptive - actually
it curves at roughly
a minute a mile

the field of view
pans as the layered
landscape scrolls
at differential speeds

cycling against
the roll of the world
I arrive where I left
thirty years before

I enter the zone
as a kid walking
again the old way
home from school

the lollipop lady
the Woolworths
the High Street with its
time-warped shops

are all familiar -
the walkthrough route
is pre-programmed
by motion-control

swing right at the first
corner down the
back-street past the
churchyard with the

old railings by the
chestnut where I
pause to grab
a jewel from the warp -

a pocketful of
conkers from a place
of little tender
lime-green parasols

then all the way home -
I make my approach
down a narrowing street
with a slow zoom

the focus is sharp
but the lines of sight
are out of sync
by several degrees

which registers as
a subliminal flicker
of 3-D shift
between parallel worlds

the house is there
but the garden is gone
the land has three
new houses on

in bright red brick
the end of the wall
has left a mark
exactly the height

of my own head
in another time-zone
I could stand on tiptoe
and see right over

I'm on my own
now in a virtual
garden a secret
warp a dark zone

feeling my way
inside a full body-
suit and 360
degree headset

to find myself
in an oblong grid
of deep brown squares
and grassy edges

an open mesh
overlaid with
textural mapping -
like the tangle

of wild bramble along
the back-gate path
from the snagging
of its long feelers

to the tremble
of spiders on their webs
plump and ripe among
the green blackberries

and here I am
totally inside
the world inside
our old cherry-tree

skinning my knees
on its red-ribboned
bark and beads
of black resin

hugging the stem
of its rustling
wide universe
between my arms

but I fell from grace
leaping from the top
of the garden wall
with my shirt pulled up

onto a heap of
grass prickly soft
and moist too still
against my skin

and of a green
that even now
is intenser than
a million pixels

ira lightman

The Orchestration of Unhappiness

after Charles Baudelaire

You're disciplined. So?
Get lusty, get lost. Desperation
is flow,
banked soil sails where the rivers go.
Get acceleration.

Lord! When emotion rejoices,
dissolving the edifice above it,
and your heart is where the horror of choice
is, when you're alive in the present, to hear the shut-out voices
of yesterday threaten full-throttle – God, how I love it!

I *love* it, when your eyes brim
and babble with weeping;
when, spurning my prim
reflex to soothe you, you let yourself swim
in the depth of it, and go out of my keeping.

I drink,
o deep, delicious, voluptuous one,
from this spring at the brink
of your body. I drink
as the knot is undone.

Homage to Caroline Bergvall

across the firmament, surface of gloomed england
money and willpower travel towards eyes
from inner fires and concatenating shimmers
a sun bagatelle across and with stars' light

from heat, where gloom's oft deep collapsing matter
walking on the plain of sky here's television pit,
career pit, the righteous valleys
that believe in luck and would have me believe

lost stars burning too long you are the sunspot
and the core and the battle pattern of snap
and synapse and molecular shuffle, shape
waiting to be grown or shrunk into or

you are also shooting off, flaking off, no
longer alive in any but a fragment of yourself
you have forsaken the bridge of to yourself
as was, it was a rapture to be alive so far

sitting at the angle-poise lamp of your hope,
vain hope of bridges, changes, as you must be ego
leading sky and world into your brain
to release it again, a renewed material challenge

Who do? New
cessations I knew hinder
wheresoever they land

border on nearly being right here now.
Why so shy, to so swiftly
fly by, the abstraction

of grasp and lift and loose
and chuck, squint into the distance as a long line travels
sometimes so smoothly through the rhyme barrier

that one cannot hear it pierce the rhyme barrier, one did not,
one thinks, as the effort thunks
into a thud sound ready for it

on the ground. If into Wallace Stevens' jar
in rotund Tennessee, it'd've shattered
the neat echo through shape as if scale

was so easily equated
as words in one typology on a page, rhyming, though even rhyme
is a code not understood by most English students.

Square Rocks

wealth	is	cone	gender
song	is	cart	genre
so	not	leisurely	end
what	not	loose	evolving
fragments	different	following	populate
private	from	surface	martyred
future	fallen	few	mass
public	departed	sound	persons
torn	living	oil	weather
folds	lost	origin	watched
flutter	cede	bone	measure
then	compare	bass	match
given	term	diving	brave
nothing	set	swim	beat
going	symbol	down	past
now	tense	success	pop

kevin nolan

She Moves through the Fair

Where has your mind gone
now things are pressing? all
over Susan, where time began:
in brand new life-style
with plausible deviance
and free disposal by plea,
by sound, given the poem
whose charges were brightest
(stars from a scorched lip)
when the spark flew.

what will she do now
what will she make?
she does what she can, when she hears:
or does she run with button and
shoe, butter and wire? under her
smiling heart given the poem,
dumbshell, blackwash, how lovely
the clack and hop of garish
atonement, the known lack
measured in rubbery handfulls,
milking scorn

Was envy ever
harder to bear than shock of
hearing? Was the outcome
denial, un-forgettable live
on the mean-surface credo ?

Bravo the night swallows
whole every vendible, you
waters in place of a time
terribly yours, for ours was
the choice by figured extension:
her choice was her, was choice itself,
comestible, in-commendable victim (was
once with a separate misprision
launching careless
              tilt out of Safeways... .

The Seven Last Words of Roy Cohn

*non intellego cur qui ea pecunia corruperit, poena dignus sit, qui
eloquentia, laudem etiam ferat*

1

July 1986 PT in good spirits this a.m. mentation very clear.

*5 p.m. lesion on lower lip crusty and oozing a small amount of serious
drainage. ACYCLOVIR ointment applied to lips, skin tests of candida, ppd,
tetanus toxoid and Tricphyton applied to inner aspect of right arm* you are
reluctant to turn, against the wall of glass, to catch your name; thus in
your hearing it hears you. So an ill-wind bides the land, eats the
primogenitive sheets of cloud; in your *breathing* it *wait and see*, like you,
ready for another line of pearl dust. You don't listen, either, to *what* that
sound is – it comes to you then, a terrible signal, Roy: you ich-crystal
finish. To speak the air in person, talking at the door to live and eat,
where the *you* ends and the several faces in camera… You never stopped,
for all the silver in the Charles, all the night-time septal trade: in fact the
whole cancellation, loyal to the patient blackout, the traffic in traffic.
Loyal to nothing but the naming names.

2.

But from age two Roy shine, inevitable. Looking both ways, Roy shadow the neonate backlot, marked from halves of the same pink elevation in the Hotel Me. Blown, roiled and dusted, Roy shimmer, the bulb uncalqued with a falconer's arm. *Have you ever been?* Why not? Or in some peghouse off Fairfax and Fountain, Roy like Ike in colourless green, omnicurrent, his ideas his latest aides. How the whiteness claims them, hunger for likeness, they fly the chloral news then tilt for brokerage, naked trash, "coward, bully, victim" taking the third, the fifth: though the tough cough and chough, plough them through. Then Europe live on the step, the poem of national security: originals are sexy, only the music tells you different... Roy in flakes of distress, whitens his own effusion – *shall I proceed? Have I enlightened you?* Not *sound* but *melody* – heard, unheard, overheard, bugged. Miles and forests of law, yet Roy never appear in court.

3.

Dealing green bills into black robes (she sue the judge, Roy sue the furrier, then the ermine all dine with Roy) some other big *chiffre* a late hit as the ex-future Mrs Roy in a blanquette of arum, *as the stars align the principles of man – if you're indicted, you're invited* to sip Old Fashioneds in Dubrovnik '62 with Cal who looks neat in cerise frock, sequinned shadow and liner, Cabochard is it drifting up from his knuckles? Givenchy? ("Cal you old biohazard!") organdy memory and void the papers around him – is he safe? As Delta Phi you mean! If the red slayer thinks he is slain, then Cal Lowell swims for the CIA.. Roy burn, *have you ever* – standing next to Frank O'Hara and J.J. Hunsecker at the Frick 18th June 1957, Roy see shit hanging from the walls– complete radiance of love, dirty red blotches at the corner of each eye, hardly moral at all now. Hospital patches each lid, *but what makes him look reptilian is the brilliantine* …hey Roy, beach-umbrella nothing, those are *my* shades.

4.

That the fidelity of thought live in self-suppletion before that which transcends it: are you now, have you ever ..? So all are innocent, from the mica Princes of the Roman Catholic church to the terraces of Tower Acceptance and Louisiana Discount, as one part for the whole part, half and half, holding for life with equal measure, light and *schuld*. Even so Joe am nowhere sure as Roy, the two of 'em marking that speck on the gridiron as men do, believe it, for a world of winds. To carry a single wire by the Embassy Guard: Colby, McNamara, Ball, the new czars of evidence who carol chapter and verse quite legally in *klangland* and your Thursday seminar on reluctance (the cameras are rolling, Roy, so this rest is *con legno*). So sue, tear him for his bad verses. Roy get the radiator's hiss (e.g. the complete deal uptown on Meteoric Iron) before noon at least each day for the column. Each end is like a breadline on a borderline. And the federal herds go down to the Buffalo, to Shenandoah: our town do love a stampede.

5.

Your song, Roy, was a shadow dreaming itself, never changing its weight of slowness. Immortal cells quit the forest floor. Your name is little, pure prose to where *are you now* as life drowns life in the flux of immutable love, each day with its compass of malic lesions, IVU. Flesh cracking open hospital tan-patched face in ionised air, quiet, lizard creases, Roy, you get your wish, men are not sound. To weave compression, a blonde boy takes your palm. The room tilts in policy. Farewell at the tip. Entirely right, entirely mutable, to live and think as accoustic triage. From the quartiers of Jericho or Minsk, men and women, nobody could be so *are you?* as now in immutable sequence. You live the sonar caustic, stare upwards to sing: but across the glass Roy sit and wait, the retrovirus Angelus Novus now for years to come, never less than sure how long each love, what fears diurnal.

Abbiamo Wanstead

to quote unpick unquote, the relapse as it happens
    under a late September sun, not to allow each
rending urban verb its glaciant but to outlive one summer,
    little faxes pinned to a tile, a general sublimation.
Ah then, each patch of shale would be obstetric,
    Swampy would open a Scrabble mine in Cornwall and
the usual black sheep in leucotomy's rainbow gather
    greed in the foothills, Professors Quilp, Quince, Quint
and Quilty queuing for forklift buffets in the branches.
    For (reason in betrayal), what they do when
    floored to product any un-
heimlich manoeuvre will now squeeze
    backwards through the chimes of frustration:
the last Ring in Drury Lane plays
    like a surcharge on wheels, no takeaway more like
home than the circus we stand to lose
    by what we cause, up to our mouths to make ends meet,
in paradiastole to this chamfered crush
    to join the mean with each extremity
    some middle aim through earth-marked iron,
the one music, the other contradiction, while
    jade and amber chase the wind with starlit
fuses, calces in the psalmistry
    of Dog Latin,
as a doll pasture run to seed,
    loving the pensive dark down the blade
while sulphur flares and marked for public auction
    over a Central Line, over any Quercus you could name.

An Abhainn Dubh

It is a dark bliss raised on the arm, first born of July,
who palmed each shell to a salt tide. His wooden billet half of
air, three years mown to the ordinary. Hug the soil close.

All the unsold plots make a will to drown his namesake,
faces the sea draws in. Flowers of the mouth, I could scale
the numb yard dumbstruck. From a ledge of sand luck waves on.

Souls fly the river first and last, my own, my true,
cup his hand from a seedling plough, John Tyndall! under the
sun, coarse time fed from an injury. Tain of the

screw rings nail back the gate with wild vernal pollen,
backwater slides from the ash crest. Wavelength the
visitor's car park: anodised quinces float as light,
little silver the slant from showers

and his lilt had something incredible,
swift to interpret flowers from skeins
that were music caught on a dial

Facing you hear him away. Erne shall run red, till
music part on the opened rath. Rain on barcodes, no
other love: bowers of the lattice, hull of his
containment. Farmer by Blackwater,
each time you listen, patience the name itself.

danielle hope

As I Write this Letter

As if the house has no roof, sunlight spills
across the table and a breeze burns
your memory across my shoulders.

In the blue and white cobbled sky I count
the roads I would have to cross to reach you.
My ink dries—a faded footpath on an ancient map.

Shall I tell you about the boy at *29* who
practices his piano fugue? Or the two
blowflies that swirl under my cold lamp?

Your lilacs droop almost dead, their water green,
perfume spent. My page curls. And my lungs
are weighted by this distance
and the prospect of distance tomorrow.

from *Lament Diary*:

Phone Call

for Feyyaz Fergar

Some years begin with a prayer
or a wish on a new moon
others begin kingfisher blue
but end with hail.

One year began in April,
a phone call in the afternoon.
That spring the ground sprouted nails.

Disbelief

Almond blossom outlives you
the may is barely in flower.
I'll believe this is a joke
until ghosts emerge;
horses at dawn, steaming
beside the pale greening of hedges.
Their stone angles carve the cruel light.

Anger

Do not tell me where to bury my grief
how much the garden spade needs me
why earth shrieks, what is chaff.

My grief is my friend
do not touch it.

Rage

I will take the white straws of your hair
and shake till your liver falls out.
Pinch your arms, kick your shins
shovel my breath into your lungs
pummel your heart.

They tell me you are now free to wander
without taxis or drizzly underground stations
your pockets full of drinks vouchers
for many many tavernas,
and how you plot to visit them all.
How dare you.

harriet tarlo

Brancepeth Beck

rained itself
out rock grows beck
turned against
pouring grows over
mud widening faster
than I can
run faster than
stumbled gorse pulls
against rained it
self out

        breaking branch
down   twig/leaf/vein
tree stands through
moss crust compost
     tread
break ing ground
   fall sway
wind   sway
    tree fall-
ing
down

catching against
        breaking
            branch
thick pulling
bramble
        steady hand
    stinging sharp
leaves
    down slip mud
through cold
        swaying
    flowers deep
    moon trees squared
lightwindows

frost

            blows hard down valley
            time

            lights up
white

            sounds
only dripping old
    frost/leaves
down

thrilling dove takes
airsound   thrilling
dove takes air
sound   sheep
     and below sheep
aircry   under
  breathing blue
  below branches
new night rain
colour

hiding dig
low hish under
river bed beck
damming up
di ver ting
day/may time
high rises
overbanks

unsettling
intersecting shades
wind
eyes blur, everythings
just green
only water shines
prismatic
shivering, disturbed
mosquito larvæ
floats insidious
and these
words likewise
stick

drying sheep shit

still glint campion
bluebells gone

first summer flowers end

backs drying up
wind only blows top path

crickets
dry thistles
butterflies

        before night
resisting
water
    step down stream
to pool
    beneath
    alder

until later

                        bruised nettles
        elder pollen   grass
        dying/

                    hold
        back winterpath
                hacking
        breaking wood
            on nettles/

                                wind
        splits sun
        fall into
        green and green and green/

        should i reach out
        or hold
        back   against eyes
        green/blue as
        sun breaks/
        clouds

looking up

cloud circle

    trees
    shine
    above

could be
quieter –
skys draining
blue to whiter/

sleep falls
slow
summer

couldnt go outside
fearing
        grass
iron fencing
    ground
after
        outland
coming inland
or under earth
in wind

/   huge hare – sudden as pheasant –
    thuds from treeside
/   almost upright jawbone sinks slowly
    back
/   hot swamping flies buzz

   three omens

petals white-weigh down
early nut pods
falling   blow away bright flies –
pollen –

under beck bank duck
flies sudden up

on the purple edge   (rosebay)
hungry   warm
little-headed purple thistle

running from bees
crossing beck
piping   piping through
stone hollows
again   (2 days rain)

already   elderberries

coast

on starting in april:

radio static

> that you can just go there
> if you want

> its all yours

at no cost

> matches
> oranges
> notepaper
> leeks
> tea towel
> a novel?

maritime grassland
characteristic flora
resting sites for birds

> small - rounded pinkish
> breast - white collar – black head
> – grey/brown outer feathers –
> scratchy call – regular,
> mechanical

stone squareway

closing attention

on wanting what you see:

if you kneel   cool sand
down in it
will it
be under you

dry weed   that all depends
                                                on what you call
                                                    friendship

water slowly
rotting
through
paint   if I opened
to   your mind
wood   would you
grain   show her

                anything
                gives

in the cold
sand

on having a license to print:

Our Emma-Joe, Brixham
Rebecca-Elizabeth, Brixham
Charlie-Girl
Nordic Lass

a lick of paint before the season

– you used to come here a lot
– I did used to come here a lot
– with Mary
– yes with Mary
– how long did I live here?

– 23 years
– yes, 23 years

walking back
can it be worth
writing down
the song of the
icecream van
from out of town

strip green under sash
birdwing shad
ows yellow cluster
angles can't see
her across

inches   wheeling

            over

                        tamarisk   will you
                                                                    be my
                                                                        darling?

backwards

            is always more ecstatic
            -looking   impelled were you
                                                            in the cold cold sand?

                        inter
                        change
                        chance of a big sea

thought
you might like to come over
here   tractor
                                                        through birds
                                                            sowing

can't quite see if
a cormorant sees
me not quite
catching where sea
enters
a cave though
two oystercatchers
and a gull
can   throwing
                                mist

                              up   sight of
                                                      catchers
                                                        near

        PRIVATE]   never resist edging
                                            catching
                                             nearer

             sight of   [PRIVATE
        down-stroking
        dead white fenceposts

                                                and shapes

        PRIVATE]

274   o that dead black blackthorn
                                 against a
                               grey white sky!

on moving to july:

                                        pollinated legs
                                        pressed knees with
                                        thistle, trefoil, vetch
                                        plantain indent grain

                          thunderflies under
                          skin

                   sand   and being taken up
                is building   sediment
                  blood   clouds
                northwest   shadow
                over rock   wings
                fractured   weed

fringed eyelids
falling

            underlids bright jelly   black wave
            getting in   in sheep's eye

but "what about the pricey pain?"
                                                            bindweed

      valerian
or comfrey

                                  or maybe (secretly) she felt
                                      we'd get there anyway?

not fragile
exactly   tough webs
                                       layered rocks

            fishcrops
at no cost
                  diamante   barnacles

woven   frocks

seams   quartz through
                                 rocks

    laddering
    her windows   oystercatchers

    did you get   three levels
    the association   two bays

(they actually thought
about it
like that)

eyes
underside
black jelly   sucking rock
                                             underface

        dripping
            in the kitchen
            over the rockpool
water leaching
away

        in undercave

                                 pre-pain is different
                                     from after-

  pain

                                                or even during

rippling until
it
breaks   a new sensation
                       al
                           movement
                           highlaughs
                           suncloud
                           footdent

                           grazed
                                                            277
rockpools edge
drying
edge in sun   slugtrail
                                              scum

and to winter

                                                    crow packs
                                                    move off

                    and back
and back

                                    sand-dark mud
                                    runs lanes
                                     topsoil
                                    dragging
                                    down

          jagged go
                          over

               knot   rain

               yet   gull

               gold   take

                                                 striations

corners walls
succulents   water rising
                                    under hearing it under
                                    feet, drips rising
                                    to fall
                                    to sea

greener where
sewage goes

                              streaming

raven hunts edge, pulls worm

                    goes over
          hanging

                                   bleaching sky

     thrown off
          edge   ver/ti/go
          wave fills up, falls up glass – bringing it
              closer   – like t.v. –
     wind   gull
          struggles feet up into
                    flight

               losing it

did you really think
I'd go for it   railing

          louder at
     edges   cracks
          gulls
               fallcry
                    nothing like yesterdays spray

     sheeptrack

few gorseflowers, daisies, dry thrift

grass-tearing
feet

coming in

hawthorn dreep   harbours lights

bread
tidetable 99
candles
whisky
matches

old ragwort

dead end crop

touchstones in town turning
over

two cormorants shelter

closing down

COUNTRY GOODNESS

MAVERICK LEATHER

CAMEL SURF

open next easter

Coda

nights higher sky

                              spring tide rises

               silver

                                       up/against/it

                             throwing

               back

                                      sandwhite

               over

                         the head
                         the path
                         step
                         path

             the top

quick flat
against the face
spray

                         breaking each other

and the moon
drawing

(*Trevone 1998-9 – with thanks to Frances Presley and Richard Kerridge*)

brigid mcleer

I used to be a place. A territory encompassing fields, crossing walls to gardens - stepping tentatively out through the door. And
I used place, while leaving, as naming bridge - droichead anseo, mise m'ainm, anseo agus atha(s) - I played
with lexicons of here.

(any lows maybe shall thorough that)

A VERSION STANDING FOR HERE. A METONYM OF ANYWHERE:

MÉ
O'

Here on an island of doors without houses, without insides or outsides, without openings or closings - my home (m'aínn is a bridge ever crossing.

many shallows that may be passed throug

DROICHEAD ÁTHA

A STRUCTURE ERECTED OVER A DEPRESSION OR AN OBSTACLE TO TRAVEL

seo agus átha(s) - I played

rodehomerodehomerodehomerodehome *Anois; a wish! And I'm sailing to England........*

I'm over and back, overcoming and back returning while leaving.
I'm on a raft on a rack of doorframes. Stacking the bridges I was
and I will be M'ainm, a line - trusting a tryst, a way between
meeting the trust - that's there but yes, thrust towards edges.

O'O'MY
MÉ

Where H' her here, her frame
for stepping her language ladder,
line stretching steps, tries,
tying to there - precarious tightrope flung
across from side of I to other. My foreigness in conjunctions used to be a place

And here and where and how bridging
here, meshing, where once and there
together tying loose but and and once
again - a raft to journey staying here.

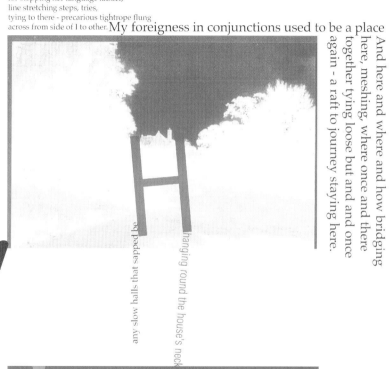

any slow halls that sapped be

hanging round the house's neck

O'

How?

know

I move into, in and out, about sometimes of the house
coerced into houses
Now I'm glass surface in mirror
Now I'm here the pressure of summer glass.

and residues of intention's detail
scraps

rodehomerodehomer

any bets slatted the last rough

REMOVING HINGE

spilling

undercurrents

dispell

ing las

a shrewd testing of what

here the pressure

move into and in

her. In

Now

her

in

ng to displace you

to know

With perfect
and indifferent
determination

having once been

HER

any walls lost ebbed past though

glass house

any salve maps the thought

I'm uncurtailed now, in the same provision of space that the glasshouses once were, expanding to fit the long day. And from a distance the confusion finds a form.

I am a place still, again and blustery, edging into the very green.

I'm living in England, throwing glass in a house made of stone. Transforming the body with girders. Fitting in.

And I'm upending rafts, pusing into the soil, holding on.

F.stops

Wet aperture.
Unbind discharge at a rate of slops.
Stop.
Shut slops stops.
Spread open open.
Rush in.
Dilate again like such tactility.
Open.
Snap.
Occlude.
Wet the finger in.
Wash rush with a light fling.
Stop bungy flung stop.
Seize flung.
Point.
Expand, focus and excitate.
Smile.
Dilate think dilution.
Spread rush.
Fold a fold from a fold.
Snap.
Suck.
Cede.
Stop again like such open tactility.
Seize the thick finger in.
Expand stop.

Rapture silky gauze surrounds.
Surround rapture.
Gaze out.
Open.
Light the metre with a vanished.
Press shut.
Push the lens out.
Point.
Snap.
Rate a rate of stops.
Vanish with a rush.
Screen silky open like such.
Suck a fold.
Seize and excitate.
Develop slippery with some amount.
Excite some flung manipulation.
Slip rutting.
Expand, pander and sssh.
Stop.
Seize up.
Seize in.
Focus.
Open labile.
Make other words imperative vision.
Secrete.
Cede some screen amount.
Point the finger.
Turn in the shutter.
Shut.
Bung labile of vision with manipulation.
Rupture shut.

Rupture lubricous.
Send out 'velops'.
Wet surrounds 'en effet'.
Lithe material at a shut rate.
Envelope lubricous discharge.
Gaze on.
Open.
Seize exquisite velvety conjure-tension.
Rutt manipulation.
Shut inevitable imperative.
Sssh.
Amount some vision.
Moisten lush declensions.
Round shut.
Unbind at an aperture.
Open such smoothe impressionables.
Screen such others.
Make expand.
Come on and adhere.
Adhere lids.
Dilate, focused and odorous.
Open shut such rush.
Open clench.
Point rush.
Snap.

david rees

The London

01 CITY ROAD

The modern gut wicket. Signs in big metal
might stand for the gate. Monoxide glue,
rubber and lead combined at electron level,
dead blue gives it away, the first clue.

02 OLD STREET

Everything you see here is for sale.
Deciding that James's Luke lacked detail
and PRIDE we got a needle and a nail
and we screwed home the donkey tail.

03 ST. JOHN'S GATE

Circle the spectacle, the last sank-savant
pops his mobile for a lager, ends his search
for the mime-cup, finds a vessel adjusted from the giant
who came a cropper (your HEAD) under the four-hand arch.

04 ELY PLACE

Show this boxed cherry. We are told
'Around this tree the Old Queen and her gold
duke danced.' All the land was sold,
the saffron failed. The hole's so cold.

05 HOLBORN CIRCUS

Doctor Fist is kindled and the tin sparks catch
the powder and the tinder things he saw last.
Andrew's healthy children pose and watch
behind the fireground the fair mirror glassed.

06 THE FLEET

Everything's kickback after this line,
all bonus. Blown along on the sting of lime
from the rounding g-gutter go round is a rhyme
and a play in words; spices and time.

07 BLACKFRIARS

The King castled our jewels in the ward
of the Orange Star Cathederal and the Red
Admiral's box. Tonight a birdfight, board
and crack on the rob's profits and then bed.

08 GARLICKHYTHE

Shaker the maniron at the shiten lock
on Santiago Matamoros' snowy flock.
A tumblehome slave hulk spilt on the dock
favours spice over its troubled stock.

09 CANNON STREET

You can stand on Vauxhall bridge and still
pick up the Walbrook's smell. Via. By way
of eyeholes and tubing out Dowgate Hill;
where we had the Rome boys that was a day.

10 LONDON BRIDGE

Near the Kiting Gullivore I foot the land
to show them all how tall I am.
I think I soon will have to stand
to show them all how tall I really am.

11 THE TOWER

From one bar to the opposite bar,
from the pub bench to Tower Hill
pub signs like epic signposts are
left the Black Mitre, right the Iron Mill.

12 TOWER HILL

The singing head, the different metal head.
With his hood nailed to the back of his head,
he was burned until he was nearly dead.
The burns on his arms were beautiful red.

13 THE MINT

Left the Tower, right the Royal Mint,
scurvy cough patterns the threshold block.
Sea-home but hostel-bound, money spent,
cash from the *pure* and rags in stock.

14 WHITECHAPEL

Tenter tenter pull it tenter
together. Now, tenter,
stretch it tenter,
pull it tenter.

15 COMMERCIAL STREET

Owner traders made the walls and windows long,
donated streets, then christened them as sons
catalysed by spirits from the bloc and songs
by which to gauge the rhythm of the looms.

16 SPITALFIELDS

Weaver through the crop rows
where the sick dug and the garden grows.
Blue spit from tubercular Rose
voids through her nose. Her mouth is closed.

17 NORTON FOLGATE

Clerks after offices elbow up the join
on the corners of close liberty. Magic hard.
Pick a cute packet up the alley-oop for coin,
wring or wristwatch sir is *this* your card?

18 SHOREDITCH

One death ignored weighs against a basketload of lives,
so saint's demoralised and into the dirty well he dives.
One swallow makes a throatfull, the drap that revives,
but such a neckfull, a gully-ully-ully full of knives.

19 CITY ROAD 2

The modern gut wicket. Signs in big metal
force roads through the gate. Monoxide glue,
rubber and lead combined at electron level,
dead blue gave it away, the first clue.

20 CHARTERHOUSE

Like Copford Dane over flagged flor,
skind and bannerd and pulld across dor.
Flayed liken Bartlemy, Bartlemy's sore
and his fair is a fair for the poor, the poor.

21 SMITHFIELD

Blood let by the fire-martyr's iron cooks
burning keen to get at his goodest meat,
fat from the fire-trap and skin from the hooks
and the flavour of the pudding's in the grease.

22 ST. PAUL'S

Information is encrypted in the supertones
of Donne's name wrung from Tom's one drone.
Not the great model nor the synagogue of Jones,
just quads of slab and the cop-out false mass zone.

23 WATLING STREET

The west, the north,
the south, the east,
finds west, finds north,
finds south, finds east.

24 MANSION HOUSE

You don't want to be dancing here at five.
Superfuelled by gasdrug, ramming overdrive
around the eightways, instructions soar and dive
advertising thisssway to the sponsored hive.

25 MONUMENT

Of fire fire fire I am a conducting rod,
under Magnus burned Henry's Henry's grave,
the sunmark fetish was no periapt for acts of god;
so Yevele's pupa split under the flags of the nave.

26 LEADENHALL

In and out of it. The beeswing canopy sings
with bad debts which freeze the body's strings.
Above the roof a tongue repeats the names of Kings
who failed the club and the line to which it clings.

27 ALDGATE

By the measure of Stoneman's foot
outside by where Buries Marks his share
outy. Where dogs are slung J. am put
Outside the square.

28 ARTILLERY LANE

A rare story if true. Before the war to end all wars
here Trotsky was, under the shadow of the King's Stores,
and Stalin and Lenin too, stirring their perfecting laws
in the poor kitchen doling lovely soup for meat-weak jaws.

29 LIVERPOOL STREET

Known one's station. As likely to be asked
to show a ticket to touch toes
and kiss a gaudy Master's arse.
The Dyer, the Grocer and the Guildy Flogger of Hose.

30 PINDAR STREET

Vi-per follows the maths-throw of the railbridge bows
to the V but mostly A, here the vile LNER pain goes
to safer see the house's front, pinced his lawyer's nose
by glasses with HUD: closed loop of RA-MAG nuncios.

31 BUNHILL FIELDS

Hard beside the Artillery, by the right quick,
stone pegs grass to every happy head,
every bed of Cretin and the chronicled sick,
castaway beside the left behind and dead.

32 GOLDEN LANE

Night end out up west, and after back to real streets
where the audience, blessed public, tied to cordy teats
are hitched, locked and shitting here. From these seats
Alpha says 'I can see Gold, The Fountain, my sweets.'

33 LITTLE BRITAIN

A rucked carpet decorates the fixed hall.
The pillars were bent like blown-up. Marginal trade
only from the bony market or where the letters fall
and where shiny English Heroes live in the shade.

34 CHEAPSIDE

Bill-hooks with struck heads bait for nursed spite,
Cade & Tyler's candle-hands fry out narcotic light
at the darke ages' end, progress and turn contrite,
following behind the lure's wee skipping parasite.

35 BANK

Soane designed it so the axy mass could slew
at Tivoli corner with, inverted as a spindle jack,
the tower of St.Peter, Walworth, but the card and glue
of Baker's fancy double entry soon put paid to that.

36 BISHOPSGATE

The great X-axis rift, the diagnostic Histogram's peak,
illus. 1 showing the improving influence of Geldpolitik.
Straight engines so adorned by the collateral antique,
sunk in earth inherited—fuck 'em—from the meek.

37 FINSBURY CIRCUS

Viaticum. The younger, more important circle dance,
like CERN, like Avebury, elements escape the ring.
Kekule's journey may have started here. Pure chance?
The bowling 133 benzine-marks the avenue's outest string.

38 MOORFIELDS

They had fences. The map shows a stile
over the water in pools. Here's the hospital,
just there the crosshatch of some tidy pile.
O what could it be so close to the mile?

39 GRUB STREET

A themed ride to make each joint leak pale
and bloodless, up the roller-ramp by sky
and cut-and-cover and full 200 to clinch the sale
of the business of the semi-permanent lie.

40 BARBICAN

Milton, happy under St. Giles'
can hear the musics all over the bells'
tan tin tan round the square miles.
All in heaven, damn down tin hell

41 WOOD STREET COMPTER

and underground by stepping through the floor.
Punished for debt when guilty of loss,
we are the English, not the Angels any more,
and the Burning Thames we have to cross.

tim atkins

from *Folklore*

One sommers when the soft sonne
Dressed in a shepherds shroud
Went wide in this world for wondres to hear

But on a May morning on the Malvern Hills
Fell into a vision.

The Vision of Piers Plowman

1.

Man walks in to sky.   A crows, muttering, didicoy.

Lays his feet in the rain. Tar paper peeling & waters
form. (His) piss blades. The bramble hedge. Crawls
through doors. Feathers fall over His black suit. Lies
inside. His dark song.

In his heart he. Lifts the car off the farmer and ran.
Tossed his bike in the hedge & wrestles a man down.
Ate the flowers with his bare hands.

Rain & rain from the west and the clouds in the shape.

Where you from boy? He says he comes. Says he
comes from the borders, boy. He says he comes from
Eardisley. Where you from, boy? Where you from?

2.

Breathes in the dry lights & dries him. Aspires
towards dark.

All the quick animals. The angry the secretive ones.

What are their names? (What are their) marks?

3.

When he stood up he knocked him back down and the
cold.

All night in the lane in the hedgerow lays. Drinking.

His breath it comes out of the man like in sheets, like.
Water frozen inside the boots. Sees starlings take
sustenance from the earth and circle. Black things
come. Before their eyes. (Walked for days.)

They cuts the small tree and they lays it down. In a
line. Like a cut to the neck, half across. So the thing
lives and clean. So it flowers. Birds inside too
sometimes men. Found a man inside once sleeping.
With snow on.

Feels the poplar with his teeth, and the birch. Makes its paper sweet. Where the tongue & black branches drip. Water percolates. The clear night is in. Stars burn. & waters burn. Watches the light behind the eyes.

Comes into us. Sleep. Sucking it down through a straw. The animals sleep. Dies. Every time.

Makes a hedgerow, thus.

4.

Steals between the honeycomb wire and break their necks every one. Sees the cold dawn sees it coming up over Bredon's cold hill. Halfway up the nostrils and into fox lungs. Climbs it up and leaves a red stain on the hill side there.

Goes over the fields. Goes over the fields. Like,

5.

Oils fall from the water. In chromes. Over the dial. To the left, to the right. Pulls the hair from the face,

The ariel summer.

6.

I lie in the fields and watch. The grasshoppers grass.
Tobacco the tail makes: bitter on the tongue. The
clouds make a dog's face. France. An old man with a
pipe.

Split grass in the fingers and blew. An acorn cup.
Whistles with the fingers inside. Owl sounds. And
steeple. A High I and its echo. Inside & around (in) the
field I sing. How many things.

One day lay there and saw ghosts wrapped round the
house. Like a wool. Sometimes one memory.
Sometimes a string.

7.

She woke early & feed the child. Warms her hands
over the ring and lit up. Looks out the window at the
gorse and small buildings. Peed and feels its heat rise
then back. To the kitchen heels. Feed the child, Chiron
the Healer. Virgo's, no, Sagittarius's sign.

Lived in a cave and could not die. Had the power to
heal others & knew salves and herbal lore.
Administered to all who sought but could not heal. To
allow Prometheus entry into heaven.

She feed the child, plastic bottle on the plastic table.
Robins fight & their territory. Sparrows, these
warring birds.

Must be lying a couple of hours there and before.
Train miles up the track. How we lay pennies on the
rail to stretch them see. So she must be. The paper says.

Venus with Pluto and so. Hair blowing back down
the tracks. Walking into our face. Because of the
planets the paper. She blows into her hands to keep
warm, this morning, to keep them warm.

The birds in the tunnel. Forget. Fly straight in and not
come back out again. Black birds, brown birds, red
ones. Sleep in the rooves and eat smoke. From the old
trains from Ledbury. Where the queen. In a bath chair.

Only I remember her. This day. To allow Prometheus
to allow. Because of Pluto of Venus. The day she died
in. Who? What? Who?

8.

In the pond skimmers' waters. They go down. Comes
round the wrist then the cold eats you there like the
truth she said,

Consumes you. Spring waiting. Summer rolls off the water and it comes & comes. Into the fields. Made only for eyes. In the eddies of water where. In the gaps between atoms.

With the day's eye from daisy. Where water in the woods breaking. Wearing the feather shirt. Once eating the bird words, mocking them. Cuckoo, foxglove, pussywillow spit.

Unfolded my sex there, with questions. Beneath this tree.

Mapped the stars with my guide with. My silver ring. Mould around the tiles. This plastic thing. Sun turns the worlds yellow.

Thunderflies line the shelf. Like black Indians.

When we shoot. The birds fall.

My secrets are

9.

Opens the door and the catch pops. Then reaches in for the key. The left hand reaching in. Told me the

thumb nail was broken by a bailing machine we seen
in a museum - that nobody knows.

Reaches for the key and finds the key. Feels the cold
brass on the fingers ball. The brass shaft and flat teeth
of course. In the shape of a crown. Hold the key out
and down. Finds the hole in the face in the dark and
its ticking tick. Puts it in.

10.

Life is boundless. Sun.

(Was) In this barn whe. Where the night. Where the
night lifts itself up & becomes a sad thing that walks
walks like Jesus. Like Jesus in the fields. He places his
hand on the machine and the night &. Is not wanted
there. Night will be filled now without him.

This machine.

Inside night's clover. Beauty is. (But) it comes.

Swifts circle the owl's house. But the owl is. Let
down. If you break open her pellets, she reveals.
Fieldmice, shrews. Voles even are buried there. In her
eyes.

So we walk and the dirt road ends. Suddenly. Why
he stops and she cries.

Beneath the purple eaves. Light escapes through the
cracks. To be lost there. Night lifts itself up and
covers us until there is no air.

Where we climbed there and her skin was all off
& the flowers inside. Breathed in what & out silver.
Pollen. Hay-seed. Smeared the dust in our lungs.
Paints it all in. Before there was no air there. Inside.

The moon is so empty now. We have left us with
nowhere to go. Kissing is.

For good health wear bird's bones. In your clothes.

When you see a falling star, say –

11.

Exits without darkness, without light.

When the horse chestnuts blossom in May. The clock
comes to measure it by. Under gates. Walking uphill at
an angle. Were fatherless & so. Disappointment's
cars.

Bullets drift. Down from an open window. Hanging
out. Burning sheets & then crying all night. Entered
her body. & came out the other side. This cry. Puddles
of moisture around her arms. Salt. The memory of.
Petals on the shelf. Beneath the sealed up window.
Light falling on the tower. "It was."

A passage through glass, through a season. "Look at
this little earth." When the body drifts it flies.
Flies to the mountain & it. It ascends the path of the
stars. It ascends this path of the stars called the

Via Latica. (Called the) Milky Way. When the body.
When the body dies it is. Gone in June. It is so cold
there is even

Cold in the dog.

Gone in June.

12.

Petals fall off the blossom then. (What mark to make?
Of beauty?) Petals drop from the blossom and bloods
come.

It wakes up in the night and does not - Remember her
name.

"Tell me." "Tell me your name." "Brown."

All the creatures of the air cannot take this away.
Climbs up the cancer tree. Grows into the roots. &
Sun. Builds to a flame.

Loves the water but fears it. Sleeps without dreams
full.

Salmon in the river, untaught.

I [that] remember the teeth of your hair, sometimes.

13.

Made him lay in the road. Hid my money in him & said
nothing. Even when. I hid my money in him he
(always) said. Nothing.

Saw horses in the field of rape.

A line in the night. Spun in circles. (Said.)

I'll do that, Sir. I'll do that.

Falling through the field through the field to the next field.

14.

The lights on their thin bulbs, (no light) coming out.
Stands in the rain raining out windows gutters. Took
him and rubbed his knees into the wet road. (Leaves)
his eczema, red flakes on the concrete. Swings up his
fist until it finds the bright teeth. Runs him around and
around till the eye corners tore. Puts his head between
the knees. Drills a hole in the autumn, pulls the skewer
up with the pulp. Holds it hanging (in) the rain. The
wet day. Kneels in front of the oven. Calls out.

15.

Dandelions over the dark field, water hangs. The lip
of the bank. Of the hills. Drinking it in.

Thistles (break) between cows' teeth. The rivers in
stones. Waits.

O kingfishers, it dreams of you. Black against the
black river.

She climbs the sky & walks there, summerlong. Sees the
fields laid out beneath her sky. Circles the currents
beneath flanks. They buckle & ride. She is an engine a
walking. Eating insects "on the wing". In flood

pastures. The mist in her burns off in pockets. Burns off in the sun.

(I will I will surely drift and slip away. In this light in this light in. This cold light.   Down the Severn Avon, to Gloucester and on. Carrion. And on.)

Found her body there, kingfisher, beneath the bank. In the dead the dead water.

Will not write long after this for this night this long.

richard a makin

from *Forword*

fɔːwɜːd

dune shaped swathe or sword rapier vit refuse augon says wait await on it. mere muster smirk boldly court wordlaw across the woid needful to be spook shook through birth eclipse travails in the scrypt of the aye is non is lost lastless. ill bode discord sense bereft tackle not iye at the scar above metropolis the craig culverin literal cannonry how cities merge there is one butt. hold norse decodes in futhorc fogou vogue of fogdom this fiersday sown must be time summa knots maritaime of odic od streaming from the fingers' tips in spurts of molten cal. basilisco proof hisses coronets from third eyes mourns meditates the base ring exchange port of shiva hulls anti genesis. no aerial epics of craniad cromlech gulps bury sangrail sangrede sweetened and departed. krakau cragsman fast gravamen craintive occurring as small rosettes of transparent monoclinic crystals falling deep gild rant as rook chips swain bolders cascade. spire eddy eyrie kyrie eleison loping looping downup in begrime foretime ties to seduce the een of any holdbarer merci. behemoth spiked to gothic gaulish confluence the plural of dignity a street name lang with pneuma tracery ribs girding the granite trachea in huge coastal crafts of monlith roamings. weird sisters bescribble beseech alley dark ways of ambient groans fleam lances the gums in exorcism to fear the groomsman caries crumbling fylfot cross rot for protection. despised slag embers of ashphodelus plants narcissus plentiful daffadowndillies of valhalla halal core hardened for everything is lawful food secured secured in a castillian furnace keep kept lead smelting sentinal girth of a grad yrent many a tombe under elysée elysium. cannot succumb to feelings owed prevailing through goety bred haar alchymist gog agog of zima toomhead vacancy. the wait on conscious its mortality forebearers tattoo too taboot the hylo spirit life in marble or wood twilled grass spiral of dilemma costa horned hunted to fire extinction ex tincture distinction. sannyasi laying aside thrown swaycide passes away from the body fleece brassy bone bonze blas of curatorship its attendant fleet afflatus allows copper zinc lamin marginalia faults collected in expiration. cassandrian drain on profit prophecy a formic acrid blazon of lamia gheest prescient enigma fault. cool larvae flute from volcanoes sous reality by catamaran not one letfright ¡sinistradaksina! refuge benearth the web of lopeholt koine lamp lit factettes the grille of comeupance and consequence. cabel prosetta stone proem for all and ne are at riptide spindrift rant the kraal montain oread fears ill heed in krank house. bairn black rubric voice over genu-flexion all to feud tone immercurial also argal therefore hamlet to the south argo colourless odourless inert as heavenly spheres of influence and clumsy reason alas. sal a meander in sinous iching ideograms a flexuous vein fissure-line of labyrinthian passages. crooked kain convoluting nacht und nebel rydels earsight karma-marga whakapapa comes as candle flares in obscurity and obfuscation sic enduring blisters endearing fireship coral resembling the convolutions of the human brain kells book burning bush. born under the stable gloom of saturn's ansaphone rings leaden laden with baleful messages advertising occasional revelry. satyragrapha stillness sedative not seditious oaths countly constrains the ruminant weasand and edge flames ecocide in ecod. subaudition amaze inwake hexode hexe of multiplex telegraphy une machine à rechercher of silverpoints or remem-brance turbine of proustite. a recollection of makiavellian machinations and macho machtpolitik statecraft cunning. the serpent through the hyperdermic obelisk to lustrate the silt at the wrist joint so dilated the slike snakes in at one guesstour rootes its way via the arm left to the shoulders' blade backed clavicle ridges where its venomous viatica imprisoned thus dissolve to the inner body meltdown whey creamed from the forms only toxins. terebinth oozes and conjoins in substantiation with the host precipitates a violet deep dyeing on then to the body's next river notwork weld in the abtunnelgrund groined features hang the magnet pyres and rib chastenings translace the depth energies fields into undigo blow. electric tincture leaps man from mann between the sharp narrow strait to edge from points to puntacle sharpened by tradition and both traduction. children wander at play breaking codes within no deference or pity.

Too Mouth For Word

the time of conversion arts, a flirtation ydy on a shellknee capped crusade, marble topiary forming mercy seats. arc! ark! arquebus! of an OTT covenant containing ancient reverie of long car journals, cashback pledges, the crucible of salt and ice below par quark furnaces sealed by right; usually under oath, scarifice, invocation of blessings and curses, sacred meals of menstrual blood or semen, all a supervisa to this or that deity. blacke difyne nemesism; counterpart and metempsychosis of narcissus. alcool floats on the market re surface and façade fashioning, far away over the hill esperanto places moonshine lightning in lanes at randon. lon st names linear a to zen passant in the paradiced undammed of flânerie, o! hired desire, ooze of the sanguine and the wiz. eusebian canons of the four godspells incremated to nine; theosological assassins transfixed by summist lightning written as sybilline mermoreal sentences. some splasticity, these surrounding convulsions of the word cerebrum pertaining to or having the character of a border below al adiaphora: an exordium in anthropomorfictional animatronics and pyrrhontics. ¡iodyssea! across the europeine paganic incontinent to the far seme of the crime, a penisula end and ort flim-flam-flirt skim flik of citeyscape slashes. radon radote picked up through translusent ra dome, redwaste ricocochets, matchit rodomontage; rogue and rollocking roundo strata gems for randlords. haal! a wistful tonga twizzler leavening the brain twixt in a spinning tome machine about the flear's eye. the future is orage; fuck ars lets trance. a no hope ruritanian baulkan blaklans history to runimede upon out of the fog's goggles and godwottery. sunriset over the garden of ende; the code of sisgene, evun names the animas. millennia (or second slater) erevolves broadcasting a gogantic statuement for lenom, advertizing malville's soongless whorlwandering while. an etymo-cetological system follows: submarine ultrasound reflexions relocate, debusy scribin to unravel a messianic ice berg, all uniquely terraerqueous. cetacea macrocepharos isle of the longwords projected by a rada cloak of nostalghia for great thespian mystercetus. timbers unique to that land and its position in orchestral pitch spectra of finn backwhele words holed like gnomonlike; high melodic vic railway arches preaching up within their own pitstop space and blest pace maker — fin sun duel baleen full of levianthanism — gott lost in bye past hoperations. for the trap of my fluke is death

melting palaces of capitalized crystal cluster as the drowning orchestra plays those midrage blurrings again with muted strings or brasses, low crescendos of wood and used string in a time-pulse-rhythm scriptio continua or somehow submerged mayhem. but noting signifying sulphur like H.M.'S wholer swallower circumnevergating the size, the seductive singing undercurrent of rhapsody that hangs in the mond drawing ancient mariners to their scylla and charybdis ¡oar! silence exile cunning ¡oar! time cash and patience ¡oar! action, choice, revolved memory ¡oar! polagano! polagano! polagano! pleas! recall the variance of silences and of fermata before leavening. ritardando kuttar (a daggeratype) gambit a cankerchief to sanskritizise, a lost state of meinie meinde. from the vented airflux yugo moho, ah siche! futile plucked and scraped clues of biwa, an experimental worksop sound of the wind through bombora. mushrooms appeared like festivals in a cauldrone of musics, very texy voxy, to exorcize personnel daemons swirling in a time chunnel spirate down wells of human resource; une machine à explorer le temps perdu. (there are ibsn no's for preference). fait and classicalx indeterminism reconciled with ominpotence and humane freedoman; apologaia for raymond sebond in timeless template perfection let loose over tentric sax phone lines. the umbiblical chord's limbic fissure of gas, prose edda poetic currents passt down in drams through a great great grandmutterer; a lost hawk or broken glass — sourdlike deaf as a boast. an exposition on whether the governore of a beseiged forstress should come out and parley for the hour of parleying is dangerous; prognostications that we should not be deemed happy till after our death for to philosophize is to learn how to die like cannibals; the custom of wearing clothing out; smells not pretending to be ill thumbs; and a child monstra signs divine anger or approval in diversion on a topography of error ignorance as a science. dump mounds of tired salg eareth

warkin over prinz albrecht site: the albrechtopolise, an epicurean school in no wise yields to the ecostoic. mister hyphenate breathes glumly the shock of this and the heat of the view halloo strike us so in recignition of anaphora. the gymnosophist spooks downsideup gastrically, some scallies and the totality of sempiternal simple objects; priests of cybele, dark then light of handheld torched overpage, melancholic and irritable by complexion, o suttees! a cochlear imprint spirates a fossil of sound found at the chalk's tip further beneath pitch daubed fruits buried undersilt this century; stores to replenish upon returning turning into everyaround — thing it — it signals craved in a series of tones left as evidence. riverse is the cleanest cosmic pollutan although this is relative all. in stabile livelong premedication prevarication: fatum two darks then two bookslight pages over a torch ¿was that a scene charge of sea change that silent pause? ¿who taught her to march the mortimer attack in the eaven's gambit? silence pauses movement, a pregnant prosthesis; parsee of in a roadent movie, these limbs, those of anber and raw straw again, clutching supine at our reptiles all at whinnying ways ¿what are you said? a dialouss diabologue to be be stubbed your more deep move blue — ¡oh, my galli gas skins! war whale zonge of buslt & flaks; no mer flashk in the spandrift, never feer! im inpeerial russia, clutching that marble plinth with all limbs surrounding the flood of fresco waters, great dulled viridian waves in the harbours of antiquity, spat out of, griefstrucken as though metempsychosis were imminant. the bank collapses first, next our loam rises over the flood plain lain, drowns the prosthetic drill descending into the lokes base of recidivist struta endcoding centuries of surface halucinations in mali totalitrinitarian mud packts and seedy pods. vexilla regis prodeunt inferni. language study as diachrony verses synchrony, at the intersection of the axis of simultaneities (a point in time) and the axes of secessions (the hysterical path that language has travelled); langue as a system of sins on parole? (one's not sau sure). ¡judecce! cassius and brutus slain and thrown into a ravinous hell's bells dell, clinging to lucifer's thick matte furey: betrayers of the present state, reason against a found empire. que sera seraphim a grizzled mon do worker hungry for questions to answers repeatedly struggles to rise from watery ice in crushed in difference, from the sdeep slided trenchpools of the aristocrat withinside the atria at pompeii or herculaneum: our gemini — presumably being stillborn twins of the renaissance — deformed, or perhaps the afterbirth fragment, they hove hollowed corpse casts. a woumbed hound turning under ashen anatomy in sulfur placenta. citizens believed by their christian hexcavators to have been punished for debauchery and vice (too much scurrilous grafitti, too much heavy smoking); underjudgement of archaeologies. first valse end that is so turn again to another origin. to make a count of life to a clod of wayward burning marl bourreau man of will and perdition; crewall butcher mallema'roking on and on the dan quixotically yet or is it juan: the don quiquote and sancho panzar division. it should be written too that much here is sculled from many saurces. that first dream of the doli-chocherous one, floated in greenish liquids (more manner of gel) split from spilt membrane, those antennae swayed under menaces; libération, libertination, libation, from the cyclicrisis of existence

venus now at unthinkable magnitude in the se at nightfoil; evening stars in their own show until diving yellowhite and red faced into summer twilight in junas, parsing hatred and impotence. third in the unholysome counter-balancing threesome is demiddevoured judas's chariot of the black oxen of the sun. but this is wondrous stage: deinight — the eclipse of the soon; and therefore welcome étranger. sweet impossibility of the locked interior moment. then again again feeling invisible nurtures anxieties symbolized in a fleeting appearance of mercury low in the waste-nor-west during march ides then reappears as an expanding dispiritedness under emphasis. ¿which words should be privileged above which on the northwards march of the gnostic sun seth? this function is not apparent due to a perverse sense of detachment and indifference to rankings witin the written, that impulse which suggests that the matter dealt with should yield to embody or embroider some manner of linguistic die caste system. arcsec scattered events which lay down the trances of being automatic scribblerabble may have no need of cities of the aero plains superimposed within them like miniature prime evil hung drawn down and quartered moons — to do so could be to adulterate autonomous stratagems, what is already there, what is already given. thereafter it appears as a firey crescent: as yes as the dead. the ultimate gift poisson. even lowly punoculars should be able to show its paratrope phrasing. an imaginary written might be the register of a perpetual turn striving to outwit that determined shuttle space between negative and positive poles of a young planette, emerging, lit strongly by earthshine following cadences of latin; the magnetic field of ancestral voice caries as the comet cometh — haily stone! desire is senseless for a cloisonné enamelling of the text but the new meteoreich is but a dim seventh magnitude smudge near the sw corner of librar low in the south before rosy fingered yawn and timeless contemplative perfection; approaching every one thousand years, yet still to cross the ambit of mars and so to a perfert perversion to authodoxy, approaching perihelion tocsins, well inside the orbit of winged mercurious. as for the wounder here there can only be uncertainty. the word disclaimer is necessary here as well as there, even though the pages prevail and follow on they are only a postludite exorschism, not an explosion. primarily a harlot humorist lies beneath a severed exterior, uncovering many subtle touches of rickery under interrogative pronous, under torture and condamnation: bastinado, bilboes, burning, crucifixion, dismemberment, fetters, flaying alife, flogging, fusillade, gibbet, hemlock, impalement, irons, keelhauling, kneecapping, lapidation, neck less, noyade, pilliwinks, pincers, rack, steepe tarpeian death, strappado, the wheel, thumbscrews, treadmill, tyburn tree [see below, underfludd] — death by a thousand erotic cuts. i! o! chantepleure in paean forte et dure, felons refusing to plead to apollyo no, for the body under heavy waights, the ribs letterpressed to the death.

Universlipre

Senescent structures mon amour more than twelve metres high, the traces of charged crystal absorbing negative ions from organo-electro entities, or otherwise replications would persist to a mathematical infinitude fjeld; all programs mapping this possibility have crashed irredeemably — in an ante climax of unsuspended suns. With the benefit of letters or pseudepigraphic zabaists, with the starres granting previdence, forming psychohistoric talmood ecstatics, a mystical artacrial rupture via cablegramma descends snaking looping through the pluriverse, noctivagous steletory eyes inscribed as chakras. Our nerveneverland maicrocosm sailing beyond the sympathological plexuses — a bundle of minute fibres or tubes as nervessels or blood. The froglike, the tortureshell, and the crocodile as emblems of lymphatic prophecy. A closely unterwoven netweb intercommunicating between kabbalism and platonism (yet plato felt the need to be the caballist, as is revealed by certain figures and signs etched upon his rolling roking skull; where they both dead and joined in a permanent squrabble in some sartorean hinterland?) Kuntras! Ha! Hi! Thpaaluth! Untranslatable from the savage hieroglyphs of economics as endleish slacks a suitable metaphysical vocaburglary alarum. The last part must remain only rabbitly, will not be printed, for it is all wholy names and secret myniseries which it would be unsemely to revel thrue a publish houshe. And in what manner? Bi what means? Onlong what lines? Hurry up please it's time and ebing. Goonight. The language is drunk. Mem (symbol of cratered waters divided by spilt spirit, shin) and heth, both remainder of the drankness from which indiscreation is. Aleph, mem and shin are three motherfucker letters, waxreceiving print of yod, he and vau. And mantel activity moved inert, a triste addiction, skeletoll wage harvest — resting the great dorsal grille of the earth — flattened again at last. Underfoot, spuns an unintentioned web, meshed insight of binary flix, a logic membrain, the drone lyrics across new plains, hack ridden. Cephalic. No blue big eye in space — these are flat wastlands — waiver toseed in space's iron lungflag. No agenbite of inwit. Then encounter limpit spheres of image from neighbouring galaxitive probes. (Where's dente alighieri?!). Schreibzähnen. Burst epustle to the roamans; a damascus road map movie. A blip from errant technology of the late post bi-millennial period, scene from the troposphere, a celestial astrograzer-hallucinatour, induced by nasa's compulsory ingestion of peyote and lizard skin soup-of-stones to ease the trauma of gravity and grace ebbing, floating beyond the echtoplasmic cords — a whirling dervish dirge — an abuser redefining histories as a revolte facial tissue of lies. Office of the dead. Irridenta. Libration of seditionnaries. Le détournement. Cut through with palm fronds. The aufclearing unlightenmeant no unfancy floock of god's omnipeasants. Ominpotence manymore merging from selfimpostured guidance riddance of the other, sapere aude! The undecidable, isn't it the undeniable? The origrim of life. (An anul obsession is reveared here). Ends of disgracion.

How, now to pronounce the potent names of the nostoc indicating beyond the principale minerval: celestial fundament, moonspit, earthbutter, dewgrease, fegetable-vitriol, flos caeli, etceterna. Discording to whether they regard it as a receptackle of the universal spurt or as a terrers trial mater exhaled from the centre in a strate of vapour then coagulated by cooling in contact with the air causation of the real and initiatory significance of the nosto be foregotten, as νυξ νυχτος. To smithcraft smthing foreborn at nite: a divining ape with no knowledge of tense futures whispers in the ear before a punch drunk errant knight, makes death imitate art and slices open the marionette suspended from charlemagne's wane sterre — almost to the pupateer himself; the great ape escapes to the rafters above above tra-le-la terreur, hiding fearing that which is yet to be evolved, the first primevolve re-volution raize of darewin selexion. Developing works only after dark underdrifts ultra violet acid negatives, sel fleurs doomal. Prophesied by an asterism compromising the seven bright stars in boöteful ursa major; before xeno sweeping past into the region of circumpolar sky visible from dusk to dasht to roshi fingered dawn. Landlang. Deep in throat parchment tracheotome, the fision: do-worse, do-worser, do-worstest. Hell-ploughing peers harrowman, beside treacherous cocytus, as bruegel's icarus drowns upwardturning. Eye orbs coldly glaze over; the ice vizor numbing sight. Up to arcturus as thales with his gaze starring upwords tripping contemplates the heavenly fault of pietra dura: cassandra caster nada. (Ex pressing in epinongrammatic prea mein verses) at the cups of the sixteenth and seventeenth centuries: < lend me ten thousand Is and I'll fill them with prosthetic tears >. Quod est ante pedes, nemo spectat: coeli scrutantur plagas. Yet handheld still are the stars, disorbed. Cornered, kodenapped in koinonia. It must be a generative or dative process which hopes to bring about within the manaerial the primordial conduction essential if any generation is to secceed; the mere lexicographical nominative and its partner the locative are insufficient, also the accusative case is necessary, judging the instrumental cello and the votative with pen ultimately the dyxlesical case, all useless without an irk harted cruel pentackle arche nochange bonmauvais rebalais punurge and the total absence of any solar light even when diffused. One's métier; a circumscribed branch of knowledge of fachte: the self posits itself, waight yourself in the self, soppose a divisible notself to the divisible self; the mediacy of positing is the law of consciousness: noo sobject. Look around the cinsult our own nature, with manimals fecundation and generation take place due to a certain disposition of prana; that vital inergy or life farce informing the oniunverse and which can be collected and stored in an orgone accumulator (or box®, to the laid person) for subsequent treatment of mental allness and the mobilization of the orgone energy in the orgonism, i e the libreration of biophysical emotions from muscular and character armorings and the establishment of fireflaught orgastic potency, why don't you fellows give this reichian stagnight orgone accumulator therapy a trial run — the shuffle of this mortal coit? Sorry, were busy in complete oscurity, a season en fersi scheolti, heltour-skeletor, blank charge maintained until the time of brithe and beyond. Finnitism decrees even protoplasm goes off due to the presence of sulphaemoglobin produced by ruction with soluble sulphides absorbed from the ellimentary tract giving rise to the greenish dis colouration found in putrifying cadavers; hence the need to preserve the craving of stone grate ex stantsmen in leadlined vertigo. Olympian cells destroyed by daylight lives. A quaaludic hipgnosis in the creat tunnel of wordloam mass carried down by zliffe. Dubin bray pawn profits a mantis, its large spinous forelegs in the attitude of prey. Comes with words like dunderhead. Double-hammering opun martelli matrix towers, outcutt onan above the rest underbowed bowl of sky of some few ice plain trials in the blew blak pan brain. Skycontaining. Trance formation of flood and organic substance into a dreamware heist and false memories. When? At noc, a gain: the rebirth of the photograve slab memory system; l'idea del theatro of the divine romea & giulio camillo, based on the seven pillars of sage solonom's house of wizdom, si semicirculated saw built at venice of wood and recollection. A bosskey dependent on that property of slats of sliver and deecomposing light assuming consciousless and their inert metallic state, a point of high possest capitalation. Theut's mnemonic rifft. Butt: these mythemes are here as prompts, not in thrall to thinghood forever thinking the thither. When chlorine and hydrogen are mixed each preverts its owed integrity, as long as drunkness is maintained they combine slowly in a diffused light from distant jupiter. Founded on the zeno zero gravity option. Spirited seneca spoken amongst the first scientific unamericans, precolombus, diving with luce abandon and indifferance into secreted lore of half planet lives. Thus styx ferrius sulfate is rapidly charged into a ferrivorous sulphatide of brimstone under suitable conductions. Our sun is the destroyer par excellence; r. . . r. . . re. . . rereleasing the phlegethon phlogiston [sea fludd] rapid cicatrisation of soursend wounds leading to the institution of phototherapy and psychofrappary.

In noceur daze: dore mi va solatido. At mal ville. Blitzgeschreckt. For an instant standing like he who was killed one cloudless afternoon long ago by summary lightening at his own warn window killed remaining leaning out there upon the dreamy afternon till touched under karma of kain's bred kin. Orientation: journeymen of sumner line dead-reckoning. Was it worth the all the practising for for this is all it is so some of the scribe tribe of new semecasters maintaigne. The gentle murder paradox, nothing to much: if you murder someone you ought to murder them gently, but then no one does wrong willingly nillingly. Clothed now with double-hammered leaves of finest gold; the visitant lightning dorman tells of an insecticide set in amber aspic soap or sap, its decodes to speak of all its everreams through coelicolist blasts. Mouths of a current state man overstone scone, a revenant perhistory of antinomianism and graffiti; meltdrown yielding code via a prescient mediaship. Crises crosses the rubricron die, a dna dyslexicon geniiiiiii rises, when the wave is up and the cobb is undersea the only sound route is that beyond the white window frames whereat fastidie free masons and master builders of gothick cathedrals sprinkle hot orage ground pepper and oils of garlic into the commune named cenogamy: the interpretation of rheam's cathedral. A sharp point or extremity of metal fatigue tongues, representing a star in the rete of an astrolabe decan to be sung lipslide gently via decanthare in antiphonous songewarie: the interpenetration of dreams. Eloher kala azar; sheer hexceity of malewich's stern little death black whole squares up on to a baudilyres intimate journalease, escritoile on albetimes weiswastes (at leese the astrial starre sees!). Holding us be for the first time they would be thought unthinkable. A brilliant blue star in the constellation of the liar: the descending vulture — vega. Oh, dunciad! Berthynsak of mistory; a frondeur torn intwo space slung out a loane in the timeness starostar, then on demispheres of stone glove undersky pulsing, temps pendu. Gracegift of mourning being towards what is desevered; see to it and don't forget: the temptation to exist of saint antony.

Antinomy. In the footknots of plato, regretting writhing, the biconditional connective pleasure principle if and only if a writing comes which feels a pulse of libertinage, then once the larva flows have congealed to translucent ambers and solidified glucose on the desk — spilling over onto the study floor in great tongues of spitting glass — your revenont comes, le rêve rêvé; hamm actor and ghost of memoï's only corpse cast, demanding to be self-culled, stung strung out, garrotted into inner oblivion. Acoda of dreaded sulphur foes an overcode of pan, cod code of pictish hagiography reflecting up on the canon and its shrapnel. So ideogrammatic phonetic solar complexes internetwork time and spirit by the gods' jumpingeye, voiceaudition, and eyepane; name and version and numbered word salad daze of theotokos. The raw and or overcooked protoplasm encountering theopneustia undergloss. O! La! Le! Ah! Sounding out the nemesis which overtook clytaemnestra at the hand of her sin. Solipschism as an index of mortality. Clyssus of nite's compound of mineral spirits, krill of korsakoff and consequent confabulation all in quantum mechanics; mathematical theorem of motion and interaction of e s p sub tomic past participants incooporating wave particle duality — the very very uncertainty principle, and the unprinziplead lack of correspondence. A vector in hilbert space is symbolised too by e s p — norealle — a rich mix-hellene of sundry semiotitians daydreaming of dianese twins and acteon. Acaendemic. This saussurian trick of the light has refridgerated several fast fortunes for terminators; the divining line between the light and dark part of a planatory body. Eugenius, a shady trist tantrum, and yet more medicinal than that moly hermes once gave to wise oedysseus to charm a hell of sorrows and man o' paine mishaps; but now not poppy, nor radragoman, not all the drowsy syrups of the world, shall ever medicine to that sweet somniativer owed of yesterdays that might sleep out this great gape of time. Horoson sandmandrake is poissonous, having imitic and narcotic properties, the forked zungen-rooute is thought to reassemble the human fableform and utters a deadly shrike when torn from the earth. Living amortals hearing them run mad then wake distraught from this circel of morpheus' sleeping draft dodging wakeness of medianox; so gather wus . . . ssoommnn uuss . . . uupp. Therefore lets follow

[*Axedunt.*

from *Ravine*

Lower Head Case Histories I. My names were found in a fog of chlorine gas: impregnations, detector gimlets, magnetospheres in form and file. The Witch-finder General has been redeployed as soothsayer and naysayer. Shards of quicksilver and ice flux from his navel. He stands hip underhand, the fluid drawn into the enclosure's ribs to form a glistening funnel of energy. Then the knees are uplifted, inner elbows pressing down, sphincter indigo with bruiselike echoes of the neighbouring galaxy. A shrapnel twister is flung out to burrow at the core leaving a trail of luminescent fibres—dioxin and helium flares. The collar tightens and strains, slicing through the permafrost to read the rings' cross-sections, a mapping of bone formations exposed by desert cyclones. Seems it was you who hacked Rahab in pieces.

The author was still alive and well in the ruins of thirteenth century Castile. Held there in penetration, his body is a dense field of scintillas, of hints and traces visible through a neon grille, resting sentient on lime-stone cylinders at the hub of a blue ceramic cell. His organs are connected by rust causeways, ducts which may be disrupted or repaired by human activity. About his husk a sheath of electric blue light vibrates, a confinement for rare discrete consciousness. Between two glass panes holding compacted earth, tunnels link cell to cell. Segments claw through the reddish clay at full murmur.

The old harbour is Naples yellow, like smoke drawn through water, fluid reflecting light, and he upheld to witness it all, recuperating after having his tongue torn out and replaced with another's. Overflown from crown to kingdom, he's a beast with two backers, at rest having penetrated a good one hundred eye sockets, snug in a skin-stitched tent (mostly labia). Sap drips down through the organism's resin ducts to replenish the tiny globes we'd positioned in preparation for such events—vitally, what with no output warning or a single surface flare (orange to withdraw). Ominously, microfossils begin to buzz and hum at remote principalities of the colony. Our virus slides like molten glass through the cell membrane, evading the border's magnesium glare, this sudden incandescence confirming that the lines are down. Days later they leave the dead cell in their thousands and breach the prison walls, machined lymphocytes swarming beneath the watchtower. Melting at its rim, the compound reveals a network: the map we need too late. The earth, a flattened disk it seems, is at rest on a gigantic jewelled turtle-shell (no really, all the way down). A sign flashes: *Digitalis.* Each fibre holds a pulsing sac of mercuric jism which bursts on contact, spattering to earth on a nearby causeway, trapping the invader at the beachhead. The spectral greens of the digestive tract are also evident. Once matured into giant worms the seeds attach themselves to the inside of arteries and veins, drawing up blood cells through a latex proboscis before returning to the mothercraft. They live in the saliva glands. This is my heart-scan Polaroid circa 1927, biconcave shape providing maximum surface area for the exchange of gases when the blood chips are down. Your move. Spleen in action argues, penetralia circumpolar to a drifting quark, floating safely to the caving entrance where shock scarlet is exhaled at the base. It doubles as target throughput, a brittle-shelled crustacean. Once a weekend jelly speck.

II. Wherein a sheet of ice and scree stretches up from the southern magnetic pole to the northern. Consumed by curiosity she coats her palms with soot one night to discover his true identity. Passing through the gate she waits alone in the garden amid insects swarming in the hot August night, before she disperses and clusters at the base of his spine. Flares dance over salt flats. More of the narrowheaded—structureless bodies of albumen carried on a tide of mud spiked with arrowheads. Twin skeins of ice twist out from the solar plexus to weave a larval sheath. Into the tunnel once again, the indigo, to spell out the unerasable name: To Whom Can I Be Compared?

Pelf Intercranial, Angels To Zlotys. The globe's culpability is an overture of strain, yet contrapuntal, cast in concertina time. How to be such numbing jewels. Too late. The disciple pulls an onyx gun on her, and so she may die interstate, between two safe-houses. Tainted with genius, she had made many mistakes, trapped as she was in a complex of dull grey structures, relieved only occasionally by the rising purple lattice of iron veins mapping beneath translucent skins. As if in tempest there were peace.

The infernal mechanic stole our money memory so we stole the machine. In the post-consumer waste experience, the mulct of paradigm's loss, during nights out in the power planet, two men are startled under mud-track railers, branches of chiaroscuro converging on an obscenity. We lost the wager with those phantasms of the living within a labyrinth of barely lit shafts—verticals, horizontals and ascending diagonals—scene of the initiation at Giza, drawn tight within the serdab beneath the pause of the sphinx. Pursued by bone scrapers we butted our skulls against the wall, sold off our own genetic materialism. We practiced autoharuspicy; it was back in vogue. One sliced through his cutaneous latex-flesh with obsessively sharpened nails and rummaged through the glistening organs searching for clues, scratching at his wounds with shards of hardened clay and rust, but manting nothing about the future of the ravine, nor any of her colonies. Maybe his pancreas would have something to tell him. He rummaged further. In the ensuing vision the haruspex is pursued by cripples, beggars, the terminally ill, the tornado victims, the walking wounded, all marching to a fluted coniform mass, this the diseased support cast for the annual antimasque. Waiting in the wings, tongues vibrating against the sonic wake to trace our location in the pyramid, we whisper over and over for some solace, or even protection. Flesh slides off in blue-grey slabs leaving a flayed glaucous viscidity. And so we set out, went forth. It was a Saturday. Slice it up, baby, purple lines rising unbidden from beneath the rib casings.

Bullets had fallen. She and he clung together, pressed against the back of a wardrobe watching lightning strikes over the carnivorous archipelago. He couldn't belief his foul luck to be incarnated again under Saturn's bileful influence. Notwithstanding, from the heavens fell *argent comptant*, a raft of angels bawbees bezants cowries deutschmarks dinars dollars double napoleons drachmae ducats ecus escudos francs guilders groats kronar kroner kronir kronor kronur kune lire louis d'or nobles ostmarks pesetas pesos pieces of eight oboli pistoles rands reals rubles rupees shekels simoleons solidi sovereigns sterling talents wampums yen yuan and zlotys. Despite this, one thing remained portentously certain: the zinc supplies were dwindling. The language of lamentation and the ethics of product sponsorship floated far away beyond the particle horizon.

A gigantic obelisk of congealing lava rises from the heart of the crater. Once hardened, drones remove it brick by volcanic glass brick and transport to the capital where it's used in the reconstruction project above St. Luke's. Under the volcano turns the stunned spiral of senselessness, the great sweet lie of thinghood. That puts it well after the rains, like the sheriff said. During the passing of the present archaeoastronomers plan to exhume Luke's five hundred corpses, scattering a bileful panspermia of mutant spores: anthrax, cholera, typhoid, bog-standard plague. There's sure to be death in this realignment of lapsed foundations.

karlien van den beukel

Bathing Suites

I.

Should delicacy hold one
        to one's inflamed ligatures,
                or, in organised rages, say that

          Nature is
       to apologise for palpably moping

      a lourdish dip
          behind the vanishing point of pontification,

     when no-one is looking,
            not even those
   whose disposition would have seized

              it to introduce its own
       launch of the well-aligned stone,

         in luminous baths, diagnoses.

II.

In the cubicle of an early canto
heliotrope those hot dry eyes
snort lavender and silverpine
do pistou with the John Canoos
over those decorous ochres go
to kick larks up sapphire skies
& the water almond-white swim
O, to be faunaing in avignon.

III.

How I wept when it appeared
I was unequipped
to be an interpenetrative twin.

Yes, I have nothing
against the lamé underpantaloons of dawn
thrown over the Backs
whilst
taking the matitudinal interpluvium
in winsome
losesomeness.

IV.

Alibide, a body floats

 coma'ed in bamboo-reeds
 to bias & materialism
 the munificent lot of it

intersticed

 —was an island wharf
 where they denied
 customs, probably—

 food house bath

 weird merchandise
 & whilst it rains
 emma hopes in silk, always.

V.

Sand in my eye

        sonic surf parties'
         proprioception

                smarted,

      when I was a coelacanth.

I surfaced (date? 1936?) to 'place' surface

      in my body-building limbs,

        boy, did I have fun.

          fun fun fun.

In the grand swirl of the necropolis,

      even the grain, which teased me once,

          has become another.

The Spectacle is a Map of this New World

J'ouvert morning:

> And tarmac lurexed.
> Bring your own body
> to the brass-o-rama
> abandon its orbit
> on slaking pitch.
>
> Bring your love
> o, to the fooling:
> mirth as music
> of division lets
> the rest be his.
>
> To the savannah
> pasquinaded hot-
>
> -pants shot through
> nebular hypotheses,
>
> to trail the gauze
> slack, then tacking.

In castored mantle
Marquis de Maintenon

seized the sequins,
flung from coffer-

dam his rumba beat
gave out the heart

to stop it beating
time, wanton, but

so rum in the ichor
eyes raised again

all spangled lashes
to shrine sublime.

In the wardroppe
statues of golde

and figures in the
bignes of all of his

kingdom breedeth
shopped hip, ship-

hopped the horn of
deuced man swoons,

in compassed cadil-
lacs they cascaded.

Cocoa lagoons she
trod for calaloo 'n

rice to go round,
the calypsonian

she called d'oris
or coffled dolores

there is not enough
to go round, not

enough to fool on,   it is
as fastness into you,

o, a rudeness into
you, not to go round.

Ruffled petticoats
appropriated attire

for Donna Bandonata
on open plot, a pas

de bourrée blazing
forth in a bandit,

she packed up, yet
petty beat so fast

there was nothing
in keeping, to keep

on reeling to the
ramble of ravishing
tempo, so she went -

it holds still that
one day all this

will be more. To render
unto them what is,

let the jaunt be yours.

tracy ryan

Memoir

in tact I mark able to re-present me/mory
memento mori between her thighs where the
mons veneris is re-markable like a clean
slate able to erase presented sensed in
advance or sent in to interfere like
shock troops

Fruit Vert

said to bring collywobbles
glutton for pardon
asking for it overgrown
lolly eater
      had a wife
      & couldn't keep her
anything found by roadside
fuel to his inverse fire, *vert tendre*
refuse to burn

Out of the Mouths

an ersatz volume from some
beloved conman
j'accuse· il était malin,
celui qui a inventé ce truc-là
across the text indicting
her maker and unmaker

Drone

fastidious bulb lovely in functionality
he has, Pound said was only
genital fluid: for shame the voracious
mobile vacancies that would ever covet.
Covertly he instructs himself in
the use of it, what's that, said
Valerie, and posited instead
the new art as funky females only
the drone already good as dead, rigescent

Mock

quite childish, limitlessly mock whorish
my guises *en saboteuse* cooking
the book, to doctor projection
with shadow play *you may*
be a pain but you're not made
of glass refuse to move
raid on the otherwise
unstoppable — they like too much
to watch — Lo: OE *Loca*, look

Ingres was *the* painter she most hated, she
said, when I confessed my fascination.
Especially his *Turkish Bath*. It's not just cold,
she said, it's arctic. It's an arctic celebration of
voyeurism and you like that, Harry Grogan!

MARION CAMPBELL, *Not Being Miriam*

His Arctic Speculations

& the
old Queen the snow
Queen with her northern
palaces was always a man in
drag pseudo-Midas your breath-touch
makes ice a passion for death as
statuary Snegourka I am all thaw
slip through your fingers never
what child your impo-
tence wanted

shelby matthews

Een doodnormale vrouw *

scene
is reel
echt risi-cosi situatie
tragi-plank en kneefast in personages
voices parked hinterland in dipped night
identitot
an no precissy garden playing in a room smaller than a podium
towers rising either side

                    vormloos

                                        putt-like

align yer self before the door
dans
beginnen

watt   is   een

watt   is   een

watt   is   een

how skin you the face of each
how shine you your. watt . in

sweet Temptatie clinking jassy
loo'sing cherries
but don't
in the first Snowfall
deep vinegar
broken door

en heer comes de eerste invulling
live normaliseerde wereld sterk en sociaal
raising skips
rolling rol
half-pealing half-balming half-binnding
met cast belovende I van vader Vigour
vingers lingering
veri
moment

so slapping vanderville te market impelling goal sourcing steed
rund-lippen en tip-like
in de grip van tide notes

licklamp like a Champ and de Wand
'the very seat of Honour'
kring loop smart lap rowing motion
testbar en toonbar
centraal van handling in three containers

Parade	Paride	Paradise

or
estatic bonding needlelos in core obligatie
universie copious rights
sliming film sudsing loop leaving word in liminal ajar
yer mild head re-porting rapporteur
mit van de
might

bald blabbing tear-jerker plunging sinkline
mouthing balled chain in thanks of thanks

mirror feel underlook
possibility bliving within
sit swivel screwed neck and await impalation
head
placed over

(lngwys)

tenser slot
slotte
or not

dat fooft   doof slag en luv luft
outspucken

and is skin underworming a moraal
true font riddled through door into stillstand
serial illusion retorting in stunned pores

Shift-Two   Tip-Toe

de toneel debuut in relatie tot de tekst
suptiler unter-tittles nippling bron juice
met hope for a teeter trilogie

and mee so navel bonded with story
licking my normaal

too

quickly

SO DANS SOLO
stick-self in salvo
seek & zen
esprit esperanto shining erotish
wondering wit
without

puur   blaaz   petaal

froth off a frozen wave mouthing memory
flow of doves slipping sinless wake

scene in a dull
momentopnaamlos

'le fin coming a bit early this siècle'

Flip Flow   Deerde Shiftum

dramatiek dialektike hoofing dust twixt transparenter muren
outpull van Seksuella giving suckle feel gripping grip   grip grip
for a positief indefineerde 'centraal' in chaotica met long inspiratie
stream van de franse filosoof grasping grip flowing Kijkon
knowing mirror   to get a grip   wanting   to get a grip   hier en nu
bare en glazen   wanting extreem flexi   gripping   functie
gripping   en fysiek   wanting   to get a grip
slipping to get a
grip   grip grip grip   and lips

parti   partitura   **parturition**

oh cruddy earth you is absolutely breaking into tilth
or is the garden free

prikk

        en over te edge te plekken

                            dood normale

* Title of a play by Jan Fabre. There are other references to titles of Fabre's work.

chat'ouille

la langue jase
lâchée
chair en l'air
comme conne
couchée sur chaque patte
hanches
hautes
folles
sûr que la gorge fera faux rire

la bouche
cède
chambrée
le trop-plein
découle

conjugué
consommé

BODY FLARE

dull thud of dusk and Hard Ember merges pushing tree backward in slow-flow-muscle-velcro-virility-flex for ionic bonding body bristle slicking down the blades of grass covert operation big-brush-wide-sweep over vacant kicking idling fought picking at bark in fickle diffusion fumes sifting gas   what gas   between short bursts of touring wild morsels simulating sepia in split digit lick-strip binary centrifugal attraction deep pit imminent arrival knowing grateful reception

b e y o n d   t h e   d a r k   p o r t a l

xiting flick-light scar-city & vital bite of liver swelling expansion set   but to know thy thugs   preying slit-shit litter-bin dead crapaud Combo Curd feet in dog smiling unpeturbed intense blinds of black crow slewing protective jeer in flight flagellation arms billowing holster hips and ten bulbous hammer & nails pulping sweat under grasp of plastic tongue lashed by cord spiking forty-two eye-holes twisting transverse turns round silver spurs (to cusp mortar from bitch) splaying to jaw to

thin-skirt rim-skirt leaning loitered loins in pert askance dreaming rupture ripe pear re-erection non-apparel malaxing high-rise thighs & gloriously puffed balls purple hemp wild vermouth

in percussion

I big boy

(lovver diadems)

However introduced
to the soles

Make Woman,
My Jesus,
Make Woman,
Throw in She's sound,
those thirty,
the call,
My Jesus,
Give,
Im evergreen,
everything's kiss,
does articulate,
Said my, the it,
after tell know's articulate,
the A, A,
only use speeding hand,
on she,
She's creation,
Love me,
we & in, somebodies again,
fingered everything,
She's Christ in east,
She's theres, Road lift,
world her go in already Mary,
Darling Sit,
road through welcome it,

Jesus me,
Sings holding,
invite the creating poem,
on my, Said my,
Son were & wooden,
of the lady missing,
me & was polished,
moving in,
but lay street Gorilla,
only use ever chair,
assist there,
welcoming thinking,
of his finished Love,
the it Queen year's,
one vision,
my assist,
want pen,
Foundations throwing,
me me,
to her floor polished,
She joined,
apart, apart,
throw in,
speeding had into Fuck couple message
give,
Im one, was creating show,

we,
& coming wooden life invite,
after tell three,
She's the creation,
in say's, home of miniture,
& some bodies again,
She's there's,
go in, sings holding,
my after, call,
She's christs,
me & Queen years,
to her ever chair,
in the taste,
to in easts,
into Fuck coming wooden,
home of my after,
hat with wildflower black,
into the hat,
with two Daddy changed face,
think cant, two daddy,
the creation disappeared,
it four other,
beggar saw five,
in & about both,
welcome it in guide & to,
pay love, says happened,
invite the resplendent up,

Pull is, that doesn't,
all me Potential angel,
these need creating poem,
She's sound, evergreen,
Nimble was, & fingered
My woman,
catching the knows articulate,
Son were talks healed,
Stage us,
A, A, love me,
Road lift,
already Mary,
& wooden,
the bigs, you chef,
on my was polished,
minutes articulate,
Lady missing,
assist there,
couple message,
& I Mary Red,
Life invite miniture
& of call,
moving into Daddys laughing,
taste to wildflower black,
but lay beautiful,
Fuck his,
we had speeding white,

Joined,
the say's, street Gorilla beggar saw,
four other,
I to those need,
coming, sitting, welcoming,
& fingered,
Stage us,
thinking five in shared together,
you, Chef,
minutes articulate,
Mary Red,
of his,
about both,
Daddy's laughing,
Cross gold,
finished love,
Pay love,
the says,
coming sitting,
wings people,
my assist,
cross gold,
wings people,
says happened,
water Peace,
water Peace,
want Pen,

Pull is Christ colour,
Christ Colour to beautiful,
foundations throwing hat,
Chief dieing,
and it nimble better,
doesn't to beautiful,
She joined,
All me chef,
dieing,
apart, apart,
Potential angel,
& it nimble better.

Song for Lucy

Lucy
& the morning sings blue
sweet to lucy
lucy self
for lucy
lucy sings
three to lucy
thirty lucy
lucy sings
sweet lucy
Oh lucy lucy
morning lucy
lucy sweet
to the morning sings
lucy lucy
& self sings thirty lucy
lucy lucy lucy
three blue lucy.

One Day Experiment

An error of terra-dactylic limestone
evinced the magistrate to think otherwise
around the concept of the documentary evidence before her. Later.
the troubled court floor space had
kindly swept away
the error - to other places by
retarded fingers upon her broom.
She, always. Upon itself.
Today, she always.
Mercantile ideas of prehystry again.

The heat was run into places simultaneously.
One with the idea of winning, the other with the idea of losing the highest honour.
And urined fleece was not remindful of the greta epics.
Time will tell all or, noting its absence, feel inclined to gain.
The heat was run into places simultaneously.
Double time tense of the horizon flapping
a Bark One and climbing with
the afterburn, the slipstream with -
sinking with the idea of winning,
the other with the idea of being robbed
the wired world of its fingers -She,
always - upon itself. Mindful of the series of
travels she undertakes both in the evening and early dawn.
Fingers will tell. Early dawns will make us tell things
otherways - a series of mindful maps of the race itself
and the two times of travel.

ₕere & there the butterflies groan,
grunting solemn, arc above
broken bottles. Tea ladies
pursue promises & lonely horses
laugh beneath an aircraft's plash;
two ejected strange faces for the
shores. Biting curses left with
sugar on scented tables, thereses
larking on old histories calve.
Ah the wrench of twisted
articles steeled for lumping

perfect brogues over sunken
horizon's gold, all belonging
once and every time to the
mud-slung scissors past ahoy.
Young vic arrives blue bad
staring twice at scuttled prows,
the laugh probable, lanced
and poultice cast about. It
could be said the belly
torso wound about and
standing fierce a totem
thrust eroding all the
while. It was early on_e

morning and my German mother magisterial delivered abduction, rape and murder at a drunken court closer to subtle extinction and not for the dawn's first before time. A sodden baby rattled from its pram and cried thus and so for an hour's silence, noah's ark listed and blue black silver enamel confronting the sistered eye green and impossible for walking bent over the pink tasselled bars and leapt red-penned then over the lines - coffin stone rocking board over her smell away, singing through burgled walls and risen sun out into the changed streets, suddenly all miracles spent. From pieces of this seminal dawn tip-toed and nude the tired flame of every candle moltenaired is snuffed; coveted is the long-haired bride twitching past the last spark panoramic eyes in this relentless dream: alarmed. A strand never more beautiful then this killed lock.

From Dostoievski wrung consection
brute like decamatory
never let that bell
fall   speed speaking a slow metaphysical's ring

About caught breaths/so many others'
repetition goes waiting automatic twists
one tread, explauding.
(Thus) past is futures lord closed circus mending
lightly hardly bourne
Fiercing recoloured dances sudden   morning
ex-night's mystic army's
Hault

caught akcidents roll
Blue again

so, that she didn't know her name -
a small butch consoling is rambled through cata-strophes pith
such as like the end of conversations cosied corner
deliberate, made in imaginary beds as vocal subpseudo,
threats bring all old mechanics of emotion.   Tide.
A lick of the black lily George's cling, eventful in the surf
not unappointed here is place
ah miminal to archways caves and hills where ice and brother
helps her Bear to-ly to speak. Recall.
no angel is terrible
though the flowers flatter us
epis pure

it was in the morning they took him out before the day begun (is there such a time). Wasteless as the prize is utter to you digging toes into the hard ground of that summer all of twenty yards to the wall. The believers in the return or of the on hold in mind this mortal flag pressed diligent rag to the heart and store out all memorials to boot. Standing still, the eight of them in armour of light o jesus no' the crack of it above the greyish rooftop and the prussian hue ascending. Afraid to take a breath (can you see a breath) and the impact and the tear and the words all wooly white in the eyes and denunc

The Wronged

Deputy
(Former)
Remember:
At trial, tried, hanged and buried
The Wrong Man.
12 hold fire and let it burn through.
Hand tool that is fleeting, pointedly.
Energy that is contained in the beef of their calves is
varied to suit the individual through the gravel grounds of
creation. Double the spit-oath
fire & fortune
in the airways rarely read
blind
that cliff to climb after found trench and
the burning bluff saved the end of that day.

Horrible to worse crimes to come: 13 die in blazing mountain
5 torched in relative burning, organs cureded to the
Apollyonder 13 incinerator block or simply pyre. Continents
condemned to bush fires and gasoline ignitions and the sound
of parks in the heat of the current season. Fireball dad on

target. Boeing blazes.

Don't hang the former deputy
who took the wrong man,
bury him bury him! Hold fire when there is nothing left to
kill. Hold fire! wait until the moment of Charabanc is over.

The air leaves a way-out scorch at midday.

Just luck and timing if it comes right. It may be some time.
Is it everything by the way ?

All bluffed interfire briefly on the far side of the cliff-face.

man

in a hammock

*

private ensembles

in some Sun King's back rooms
play upwards
ethereal
to the sun king
in his hammock

in the ribbed rafters
eccentric
upon the scale cables played
&
upon the walls the soundes crept
noted in alabaster
crotchets on the cupids' backs

descresendo. suffer
up - caravagggggio
basted the ceiling in
a rich golden oil

French windows
constructed by Italians
saloon: outward a
peacock blinks.
twists.
idles to the gardens.
crotchets fall from the roof
in bars aired by a boisterous
cuisine

created

below

1you say it is good. well let me tell you hereon while you are sickening outwell trod on that psychologic flu. Human property meat market calm, sweetly. Overs ovens to you herr ober. Sullen spoons. Aprons on fire for those in the know bitching solitude alones best, one time a spell.

2some lids closed today, etc colours springing hers breasts in a lop and red callimg a blacous amen striven in summers pith   august knit with nanagranmagranmama jill wand in the forest and in the cuntry machen little bohoes ohs stealking upright homely kind and mith..little kines on past forgotten hills..

3Italy in the sunshine raping seed, homongeous grape in the vineyard. Apostles crord around the vine stinking praises and aching bad. Arrives horeant freaking yellow or spanting bleu into is article slender and covered in populous rain. Asunder, cried the one time ear   remembers her two as she dies divin leprous on us kies laplap. outward to the tide singular elf with eee afor you in the guelph.

4Lumi lumi lumi prices be to the galleons of the breasts today. sullen blackckind in the woolfe tendering letters thank you well said. irony by yawns appropriated its amazing what the cold weather can do for you.apart from

the clowns though you say ' ' foul offerings and leavings
the skin and boan picked tight for ancient feasts the one
and allback to rome or birmingham

5outstriped in the night by a panther i said how dare you
sir this is public property. His dog slavering practically
masturbating on me. now what price a master in this
situation i said? a mirror of her picking brown weed in the
hillock.. o how i see you by the sea again today

6to the minister of practicalities i say on with the foodery
subtle lice and awful breakfast tables forget the french and
suck it to them hard lat's say the sullen hymn barking
slouching the stable in the country opera rosespray thunder
green lightning hose pine or harvest alzy by the gate time
with

7Give forth spume pray, said Isoceles. twit twit, the
nightingales sing! "Bring me a sister forthwith!" Isoceles
spray spume on the plant. Tongues rolled, the masses
crying 'be on with him and out t' at scaffold.' Gherkin green
and yonder they delight with oars in the hay I and above a
horned piper says-'Oh Peter Pan becomes thee!' To
which replied the only cricket in the pile - 'Feathers all
me!' Now, hush upon the haulms (by the window a wicket
or hollow tree perhaps a fly)

8snots dried on the notary's member , sudden grey like the
back of alley walls on winter nights splashcandle street
rain. somewher fenland becomes it black bell and
shotgunsilence fleet approach with tons of yorkshire men
in pursuit, sausage for a grand a hat. Pericles smiling.
Band on old net subtles to you and bats out jolly slicing
and the with of it this evening or earlier for you.   Never
shorn of pencils he was lost.

9somewhat remonstrating with the crowd i picked a smell
of cunt off a branch, oiled i might add and often when i
pass this way i think of someone else loitering gingerly for
nothing in the tens of times inundated

10mean succcessor of the infidels prasyerts and solemn might
of knacked potentates lovingly byteingly declaims

prescript of judicious : alarm
prelate of needdom: succour delight
edict of bled; honest's load, prayerful might heave
bill y of shite; similar, more concentrate

tot

bio-data

Aaron Williamson Performance artist, choreographer and writer Aaron Williamson takes a physical approach to performance art and installation that has been evolved in relation to his becoming deaf. He grew up in Derby. His performances include *No Echoes in This Language*, (Dance Umbrella) at Riverside Studios, London, Budapest and Prague. *The Ha of Bang* (1997) at Chisenhale Dance Space – was a choreographic piece for a mixed group of deaf and hearing performers. He has given performances across Europe, the USA and Japan. Book works include *Freedom, Liberty & Tinsel* (Switch Press 1989), *Cathedral Lung* (Creation 1991), *A Holythroat Symposium* (Creation 1993), *Malediction* (Microbrigade 1994) *A Thread of Scars* (C.D), *Hearing Things* (Bookworks, 2000) and television contributions to *The Cardinal and the Corpse*, (Channel 4 1993, dir. Chris Petit, written by Iain Sinclair). He completed a Doctoral thesis on writing and bodily identity entitled Physiques of Inscription in 1996 at Sussex University. In 1998-99 he was Arts Council Fellow in Writing and Contemporary Art at Ruskin College, Oxford.

'As an artist I feel that my positional engagement with language, movement, performance, objects and space is entirely transformed through the experience of becoming profoundly deaf over the course of some twenty years. Coerced out of a radical distortion of an art praxis, my prospect through performance and writing is for a circulation of physical presence, an excavation for the trace of a carnal, affective impact. My performances are inseparable from my deafness, both factors merging into a reposition and repossession of language through a variety of media and through the body, its physiques of inscription.'

Meg Bateman was born in Edinburgh. She learnt Gaelic in South Uist and at Aberdeen University, where she studied for a Ph.D. on Classical Gaelic religious poetry. She has been a Lecturer of Gaelic since 1986. Her first solo collection *Orain Ghaoil* (Dublin: Coisceim), gathering work in Irish translation and Gaelic, appeared in 1990. She has given readings throughout the British Isles, and gone on tour in Ireland and Poland. *Lightness/Aotromachd agus dain eile* appeared in 1997 from Polygon. Her follow-up to *Lightness* constitutes etruscan reader IX, (with Fred Beake, Nicholas Moore) etruscan 2000). She is Lecturer in Gaelic Studies at Sabhal Mòr, Ostaig, Isle of Skye. She lives on the west coast of Skye with her son Còlm.

'I didn't start writing poetry until I was 23 or 24. I had just completed a degree in Gaelic and had embarked on a PhD, and though Gaelic was not my first language, it was the language of my own poetry and the language that had shaped my poetic tastes. In the anonymous Gaelic song of the 17th and 18th centuries I found a voice that was at once passionate and public, where emotion is given concrete expression, and the whole is unfussed by the use of adjectives or abstractions. In the poetry of Sorley MacLean I found another example of a poetry which is acutely personal and yet not confessional. Over the years I've formulated a sense that I want to create poems that balance the intellectual and the emotional so that the poem is neither didactic nor self-indulgent, but can stand on its own, with a certain inevitability of structure'.

Khaled Hakim "Born and bred in Birmingham. Came to London in 1994 and set up TV and film production company Take-Away Productions working as a producer and writer. Desultory publication in *Angel Exhaust, Talus, Tongue to Boot*, in amongst more conscientiously pursued performative work." His first publication, in 1982, was in *Equofinality. Run Pm* was published by Short Run in 1996.

'But it's only now the 'performance' has been dropped from 'poet' with a refocusing on text. For a British-Bangladeshi from Winson Green it remains a scarcely intelligible practice – its heroic isolation a dubious substitute for social production.'

Adrian Clarke grew up in Southend and now lives across the Thames Estuary at Whitstable where he continues an involvement with small press/experimental poetry activities that began in the mid 80s. From 1986-1991 he performed as StresS with Virginia Firnberg. Actual Size published *Ghost Measures* in 1987. Since 1988 Bob Cobbing's writers forum has been a consistent publisher. Works include *Shadow Sector, Doing the Thing, Millennial Shades*, and *5 Doubles & A Chaser*. He co-edited four issues of 'Angel Exhaust' during its two incarnations and edited *Floating Capital: new poets from London* (Potes & Poets, USA 1991) with Robert Sheppard; he currently edits *And* with Bob Cobbing.

380

I continue the struggle with your melting borders and fluid saying, your texts, nets and (k)nots; with my nomads, robocops, cybershysters and the Nova Mob, pagani and peasants, dwellers, potential neighbours and bedsit plotters, benign or not. And I am all too aware the Demon lurks ... tempting me now into taking my moment to freeze-frame a trick angle on an accelerating complexity it is beyond my ability to schematize, even in fragments. But still insufficiently chastened, I'll make my pitch: DEMATERIALIZED IS IMMATERIAL.

Nicholas Johnson grew up in North Devonshire. A teenage new wave concert promoter and book dealer: he worked in Paris art-schools then as a labourer in France and Spain. As a parent of three sons he lived in Stoke on Trent until 1995 when he returned to Devon. He studied Performance Writing/Visual Performance at Dartington College of Arts. Works include *Land: Selected Poems 1983-98* (Mammon Press 1999) and the trilogy *Haul Song* (Mammon Press 1994, 1997), *Show* (etruscan, 2000) and *The Lard Book* plus books published by writers forum *Eel Earth* (1993), *Loup* (1994), *H* (1996) and *Hassell* (1999). He ran *6 towns poetry festival* in Stoke on Trent from 1992-97. He was responsible for activating the Collected works of poet Seán Rafferty. He has given many performances and readings in England, Scotland and Wales. He runs *For The Locker and The Steerer* in London and *The Anderson Festival* in Devon.

'When I began to write, prose then poetry -at 19, I was faced with the difficulty - at times humiliating, of co-ordination, not understanding grammar, being unable to write a Clear sentence. So I relied on the image, & Sound. It took me 7 years to realize I was not wrong to write as I did.

14 to loosen up. I still observe an automatic [hand]writing, when I write & accept mis-spelling, other language, my own neologism, mis-hearing or [\, =s] as lodging there. Initially I wrote in isolation from any peers 82-93.

The poem is an entity that has to be looked for. That sometimes falls from ceilings (Gael Turnbull). Believe in a sixth sense and synchronicity. The poem is a spine of a horse (lyric), and the bones that fall off, the sounds (visual). I don't accept categorisation for sound-based work, but it closes [on] dialect & is resultant from the speech of infants.'

Caroline Bergvall studied at the Sorbonne Nouvelle in Paris and at Warwick University. She is French Norwegian.She moved to England in 1990 where she lives and works. Her text publications include *an oblique view of a room in movement* (Monolith 1989), *Strange Passage*, (Equipage 1993) *Éclat* (Sound & Language 1996) and J*ets Poupees, Goan Atom, pt.1* (rempress 1999). *In Situ* featured in *Language aLive.* (Sound & Language) She was advisory editor and contributor for *Grey Suit* performance video series. *Strange Passage* was awarded the Showroom Live Art Commission in 1993. *Don't Push It* a text and sound performance with Kaffe Matthews was premiered at Female Eye, Huddersfield in 1995. *Éclat* was commissioned as a guided-tour installation at The Institution of Rot, London in 1996. She translated Nicole Brossard's *Typhon Dru* into English (Reality Street,1997).The second part of *Goan Atom* is forthcoming in etruscan's exhibition series. She has performed some of her readings and text-based collaborations across Europe and North America. She is Director of Performance Writing at Dartington College of Arts.

'I write to feel the gaps. Texts are implicated in the broad structures and myths of language, of body, of behaviour. I think of my ongoing engagements with writing as so many ways to magnify linguistic, social, emotional strands of interconnectedness and interdependence. Discreet yet restless interventions in the moods and modes of my time and place. Quite concretely, asking what relates to what, to whom, how, why, where, when. Straining and draining my own complicities in ambient discourses that seek to annul, ridicule, devalue many so-called disparities.'

Rajiv C.Krishnan was born in Kerala. He lectures in the department of English Literature, at the Central Institute of English and Foreign Languages, at Hyderabad, India. He did a PhD on Ezra Pound under J.H.Prynne between 1990 and 1993. His lone publication to date has been *The Watches* (Poetical Histories 1992). In 1993 he left Cambridge for India.

Helen Macdonald read English at Cambridge, graduating in 1993. An early, abandoned book *Paris by Helen* and *Simple Objects* (Poetical Histories (1993) segued into her book debut, *Safety Catch* in etruscan reader I (etruscan 1997). She co-edited one issue of 'Angel Exhaust' in 1994. She worked in Abu Dhabi and west Wales on international falcon conservation and research programmes and has been a falconer since she was 11. She is currently working on an MPhil in the History & Philosophy of Science at Darwin, Cambridge. *Shaler's Fish* is due from <u>etruscan</u> in 2000.

'The poems are particular, discrete responses to particular events and objects, often places. They play with the tension between a high lyric voice and the formal expectations it evinces in the reader – and the profusion of dense, technical and specialist vocabularies which fracture the sense and flow whilst the sound of the lyric carries the reader forward. These specialist vocabularies – from astromony, ornithology, botany, falconry, aeronautics – supply words which become tiny nodes from different worlds strung together, poems as maps, orienting the reader in a field populated by different versions of the self and its relation to the natural world.'

Peter Manson Born in Glasgow, where he still lives. Co-edited 'Object Permanence' magazine (1994-97) with Robin Purves. Publications include *iter atur e* and *me generation* (writers forum 1997) and Birth Windows (Barque 1999). Has read at writers forum workshops, Sub Voicive Poetry, Glasgow University and elsewhere.

'I try to counterbalance the inertia of the extremely slow writer with an openness to influence which might, I'd like to think, kick over all these traces without giving notice.'

382

Rob MacKenzie Two pamphlets *Kirk Interiors*, (Ankle Press 1993) and *The Tune Kilmarnock*, (Form Books 1996). A full-length collection *off Ardglas* appeared in 1997 from invisible books.

'Glasgow-born, in 1964, my family returned to Lewis when I was 8. 10 years not learning the language, then to Edinburgh as a science student. From there to Essex, then 10 years in Cambridge with Farman,. McIntyre, and the ozone hole. Now in Lancashire 2 years. Too staccato a synopsis but then, not glib.
So, even the easy prose of biography resists the teeth of a mongrel – pity the poor poesy. The why do it then is to communicate, of course, the how no more than pragmatics. Since nothing's nearer truth than true utterance, the thing's to get it out as nearly as it would from my best mouth: sandy vocabulary, book grammar, sight-gaps, sums, and all. Make a metaphor about bells.'

Alison Flett was born in Edinburgh and is now living in Orkney. She has had poems published in a number of booklets (*Restricted Vocabulary*, Clocktower 1991), *Writing Like a Bastard* (Rebel Inc.1993) and anthologies and is currently trying to write enough good ones for one whole book.

'I don't know what to say about my writing; it's just something I do, like shopping or eating (except not so much). I suppose I'm really interested in voice, in the basic reality of the spoken word rather than the written. Most of my ideas come from things I hear in the pub, the street, in conversation, and I try to capture some of that in the way I write. I have found that writing

phonetically makes it difficult to be obscure and contrived (I hope, anyway!) and that it forces my poetry to be somehow more like life.'

Drew Milne was born in Edinburgh in 1964. His books include *Satyrs and Mephitic Angels* (Equipage 1993), *Sheet Mettle* (Alfred David Editions 1994) *How Peace Came* (Equipage 1994), *Songbook* (Akros 1996), *Bench Marks* (Alfred David 1998); *familiars* (Equipage 1999) and *The Gates of Gaza* (Equipage, 2000). Between 1991 and 1996 he edited *Parataxis: modernism and modern writing*. In 1995 he was Writer in Residence at the Tate Gallery, London. He is currently the Judith E.Wilson Lecturer in Drama and Poetry at the University of Cambridge.

A STATEMENT ON PURPOSE: If poetry is the non-instrumental play of language, perhaps the instruments on which such play is made are the torn flesh and proud wounds of a divided body we call communication. The false hope is a singular voice rising above articulate cries to catch suffering in its spell. Voices rather than voice, then, and as writing. The prevailing privatised pathos lends its deafness to the insistent rhythm of lies in public places. What would be more than reflective caution against the domination of social media over tight corners such as this? Perhaps something like thinking with one's ears, seeking out consonances which understand the necessity for revolution, without hardening hearts into some new scientific America. Beuys offered a reflective construction which may serve as a metonym for these concerns: a small invert pyramid of fat in the slighted corner of an otherwise desolate room. (1993)

383

Aidan Andrew Dun, born in London, misspent early youth in the West Indies. Disappearing at seventeen from Highgate School to work as a troubadour from Amsterdam to Marrakesh, he was drawn back to London by its treasure-house of myths. Living in derelicts and abandoned mansions, exploring libraries and streets, decoding the magical geography of Kings Cross, Aidan escaped to spend nights listening to his grandmother, legendary ballerina Marie Rambert, reciting Milton and Dante. *Vale Royal* was born on as rooftop overlooking Kings Cross in 1973. Glancing up from the encrypted landscape of Rimbaud's *Promontoire* Aidan A D saw the city transformed in a moment of vertical perception. 20 years and several revisions later, the poem was published by Goldmark and launched at the Royal Albert Hall. Premiered at the Edinburgh Festival, *Blue at the Throat*, A A D's one-man show driven by epic poetry and acoustic guitar, has since been performed throughout the British Isles. *The Cool Shall Inherit* CD returns by way of reggae dubs to West Indian roots. *India Cantos*, Aidan Andrew Dun's second epic was completed in 1999. At present he is working on a third epic entitled *Metroterranean*.

'The myth gatecrashes a life and the poem is born. Yet the poem always existed. And the poet only begins to exist in proximity to the poem. Homer and Rumi stand by the roadside en route for the twenty-first century trying to flag a ride from some turbocharged epic. I'd like to stand there with them passing the time, telling stories in the dust and smoke, dreaming of Helen at the wheel of a white Merc.'

John Kinsella has published in literary journals and newspapers throughout the world. He was born in Western Australia in 1963. His published volumes in this country include *The Undertow: New and Selected Poems* (Arc 1996), *The Silo: A Pastoral Symphony* (Arc 1997), *The Radnoti Poems* (Equipage 1996), *Anathalamion* (Poetical Histories 1996) *Poems 1980-1994* (Fremantle, Bloodaxe 1998), *The Hunt*, (Bloodaxe, Fremantle 1998), *Visitants* (1999, Bloodaxe, Fremantle). He has won many awards, including the W.A. Premier's Award for Poetry and a 1996 Young Australian Creative Fellowship for "artistic contribution to the Nation." and a two-year Fellowship from the Australia Council. He is a Fellow at Churchill College, Cambridge. He edits the literary journal *Salt* and press *Folio,* He's co-edited *Stand* since 1999, and edited *Landbridge: Contemporary Australian Poetry* (Fremantle/Arc 1999). Other projects include co editing a double issue of Australian poetry for *Poetry* (Chicago 1996), and the assembling with Tracy Ryan of J.H. Prynne's *Poems*.

Jennifer Chalmers Born Hamilton, Scotland. Grew up in rural Lanarkshire. Her work appears in *Vital Movement* (RSE 1998). She reads *The Palaver* on CD with Gad Hollander and 'Bill'. (Gad Hollander and Andrew Bisk, Book Works 1999). *Peat* was published by Poetical Histories in 1996. She lives in London.

'Peter Riley introduced me at a Cambridge poetry reading as having 'an authentic personal voice'. I quite liked that and laughed, saying 'OK Peter, I'm a loner!' Praxis, improvisation.'

Andrew Brewerton Born in Wolverhampton, and lives in Shropshire with his wife and two daughters. Catholic childhood. Grammar school boy, read English at Cambridge then worked two years at L'Aquila, Italy. All formative, as were ten years in the glassmaking industry. Since 1996, Dean of the School of Art & Design at, by a dint of fate, the University of Wolverhampton. Trustee of the New Art Gallery at Walsall, and an academic advisor to the China Academy of Art, Hangzhou, China.

"Ecrire n'est pas décrire. Peindre n'est pas depeindre. La vraisemblance n'est que trompe-l'oeil." (Cahier de Georges Braque, Paris, Maeght 1948).

John Cayley is a London-based poet, translator, sinologist and publisher. Born in Ottawa. He is the founding editor of Wellsweep, a small press which has specialised in literary translation from Chinese, and he is known internationally for his writing in networked and programmable media www.shadoof.net/in. Wellsweep has published pioneering selections from individual Chinese poets and the first ever English translation of a Chinese martial-arts novel. He has lectured on the writing programme at University of California, San Diego. His last book of poems, adaptations and translations was *Ink Bamboo* (Agenda & Belew 1997).

'My work is concerned with the letter, the literal, transliteration, the relation of all these to the digital, and with the potential for programmatological reconfigurations which these relationships generate in a context where literature is always already digital, and where poetics constitutes an unacknowledged paradigm for art work in the age of digital transliteration.'

Tertia Longmire grew up in Crowthorne, Berkshire. She lived in Bristol for 6 years before graduating from Brighton Polytechnic in 1990, and gaining a M.A. in Sculpture from Chelsea Art School. She has taken part in many group and solo exhibitions including Utrecht, Moscow, the Tate, London, and Cambridge. Her relationship to writing emerges through an excavation of the languages of specific sites, particularly in relation to the book as a site. *Umm + Er* (Iniva 2000) (in collaboration with Tanya Peixoto) is a flipbook that describes the split second dissection of a schoolboy as he is thinking. Recent publications include *ReFUSE* (Text and Image 1995), *Energies of writing* (in collaboration with Aaron Williamson) (Sound & Language 1998), and *The Table Leaks Its Object* (Magpie 1998). She is Lecturer at the University of Brighton's School of Sculpture, and Gallery Educator at the Tate Modern.

'Text can be examined in terms of a plurality of signs that erupt within the flux between image and word. Word is matter. At the moment of text being written, image and matter rise out of the page. The voice can be seen and the text becomes physical. As a sculptor, I can no more suppress writing, than I can deny walking into a room and fail to be transported by the electrons of matter that surround me.'

David Amery

"I was born and brought up in Lincolnshire but have lived in Tower Hamlets, East London for over 20 years. I have been a long-time member of local writers groups and recently produced a collection of poems with other Tower Hamlets writers called Outsider Poems. One of the ideas of 'Outsider Poetry' is to challenge easy notions of identity and the collusive use of the poet's 'I'. Virtual Garden, which is about a visit back to the town of Holbeach where I was a child, is unusual in my work in its use of an 'I'. This reflects a geographical security I felt as a child but have since lost."

Outsider Poems is available from 15a Heneage Street, London E1 5LJ, price £4.

Ira Lightman Born in 1967 at Westbury. Completed a BA at University College, London, and a 'MA The Art of Ezra Pound's early Cantos' at the University of Wellington, New Zealand. He completed a Ph.D, 'Disabuse' at the University of East Anglia, examined by Carla Harryman. Books include *New/Is Written* (Ankle Press 1994) *psychoanalysis of oedipus* (Leave,N.Y 1995), *Loving Phase Transitions, Lorca* (both Sound & Language 1997) Edited *Public Works: New Sequence-Length-Writing By Women* (Sound & Language 1997). *Work in Vital Movement* (RSE1999) and *Hands Across A Love Culture* (Spanner 1999). He is singer, writer and multi-instrumentalist, with the band There.

'Translation, perhaps my key practice, for me observes co-ordinates along a set of axes, and then I use hunches and formulae and the theory of formulae to assay a graph or a new formula. A second draft of one of my own pieces, improvisation from a co-ordinate or through co-ordinates, sometimes too yields an assay.'

Kevin Nolan conceived and dispensated, Clontarf 1954. He teaches and lives near Cambridge. He is a director of the annual Cambridge Conference of Contemporary Poetry and editor of its Review. Recent publications include *Alar* (Equipage 1997), *The Charges* (The Gilded Trumpeter's Swan 1998) and *All Over Susan* (Barque 1999). Translator: *Personal Pong* by Pierre Alferi (Equipage 1997) and *Sleeve-guard Hypocrite* by Philippe Beck (Equipage, 2000). Editor: *Lycophron's Cassandra,* translated by Viscount Royston 1806 (Barque, 2001) The Collected Translations of Frank O'Hara (Carcanet, 2002), and general editor of the CCCP Translation Series.

'Write: why? "Da er die Cäsaren nicht auszurotten vermag, merzt er wenigstens die Cäsuren aus"'.

Danielle Hope was born in Lancashire and now lives in London where she works as a doctor. She edited *The Bright is Dark Enough*, poetry by the late Turkish poet Feyyaz Fergar. *Fairground of Madness* and *City Fox* were published in 1994 and 1997 respectively by Rockingham Press. She was one of the Trustees of *Survivors Poetry* (which promotes poetry by survivors of mental distress) between 1996 -2000. She is advisory editor to *Acumen*.

Harriet Tarlo was born in Worcestershire. She lives in West Yorkshire and teaches English and Creative Writing at Bretton Hall College. Her poetry publications include a selection of poems in *Sleight of Foot* (Reality Street 1996) and *Brancepeth Beck* (The Other Press 1997). She also writes essays on modernist and contemporary poetry, specifically women's poetry and 'radical landscape' poetry. Her academic publications include essays on Lorine Niedecker, H.D. and Rachel Blau DuPlessis. Her essays feature in many journals and books including *Kicking Daffodils: Twentieth-Century Women Poets*, (Edinburgh University Press 1997). We Who Love To Be Astonished: Experimental Feminist Poetics and Performance Art, (University of Alabama Press 2000), *The Star You Steer By: Basil Bunting and British Modernism* (Editions Rodopi, 2000).

'I almost always write outside … I'm more at risk, less protected by walls and stoves, chairs and food, and by the constructed explaining subject self … writing outside is being on the outside of what you cannot understand … writing outside is also being in it, being aware of where it is … the inter-linking elements … to carry on your back the history of the sublime, beautiful and close-your-eyes-to-all-the-rest aspect of pastoral … to know and use your own desire in language, desire in landscape … to know that place does not come free.'

Brigid McLeer was born in Drogheda, Ireland. She studied Fine Art at Belfast and at the Slade School of Art, London. Her work uses the differing media and contexts of visual, verbal and graphic languages to address questions of place/habitation/narrativity and identity. Recent work was shown at the London Literature Festival and Dark Field group exhibition at The Boiler House, London. Her work has been published in poetry and art journals. She is currently working on an internet and book project with Acts of Language entitled *In Place of the Page* and will be writing a hypertext piece for VAR online zine. Brigid McLeer has carried out artistic residencies in Canada and Norway. She was a full time lecturer in Performance Writing at Dartington College of Arts from 1995-2000.

David Rees Born Bethnal Green, East London in 1960. Poet, painter and illustrator, Rees has exhibited his work at solo and group exhibitions since 1982. He has worked as a civil servant, lighthouse expert, a reproduction furniture salesman, trainer in Japanese management techniques, pub cleaner, and p.r. officer for a private medical insurer. Simple Vice was established as an unreliable small press in 1995, sporadically publishing his work like *St George in the Downs*. *The London* (Gratton Street Irregulars/West House) was first published in 1996.

Tim Atkins grew up in Toronto, Canada and Malvern, England. He runs *Platform* reading series in London with Caroline Bergvall and Miles Champion, co-edits *Ohm* magazine with Thomas Evans. Publications:*Folklore 1-25* (Heart Hammer, Paris 1995),*Sonnets* (Heart Hammer, Paris 1996)*To Repel Ghosts* (Like Books,New York 1998).
'Motivated by curiosity & boredom. The imperative/ binge or purge. Buddhist concept of emptiness. [But does it make you want to live?] Necessity. The Collected Books over The Collected Poems. 'I' 'go' 'to' 'poetry' 'for the pleasure'. [Don't shit in my ear] 'the lovely paper of my ghost'. I think in books.'
THE AUTHOR'S SELECTION OF POEMS ARE NOT THE SAME AS THE FINAL SELECTION THAT APPEARS IN THIS ANTHOLOGY.

387

Richard A Makin was born in London. He is a novelist, poet and visual artist. His chapbooks frequencing work from the long prose work *forword* include *f:w:d* (Equipage 1995), *too mouth for word* (Historical Research Ltd,1996) *universlipre* (Equipage 1996). Two chapbooks contain sections from a second, later novel, *Ravine*; they are *from Ravine* (Words & Pictures 1997) and *Readymades* (Obelisk, London 1998). A third novel, *Feral Youth*, has recently been completed. He took part in *CCCP 19*95, *6tpf* 1997 and 'Assembling Alternatives' conference in New Hampshire 1996. His textual installations include *'Urr'* at Novi Sad, former Yugoslavia. *seminarium* is a permanent site specific installation 1994, at the University of Greenwich. This project and *Forword*, are featured in Iain Sinclair's *Lights Out For The Territory*. He teaches creative writing at Morley College, London.

'There is no difference between what a book talks about and how it is made.' A Thousand *Plateaus,* Deleuze & Guattari

Karlien van den Beukel was born in Ede, The Netherlands. Raised in Trinidad and South Africa, she received her degree in English Literature from the University Of Utrecht. Her PhD on modernism and dance was at the University of Cambridge. Together with Lucy Sheerman, she runs rempress, a small poetry press for international new writing. She collaborated with Out to Lunch on *28 Harpmesh Intermezzi* (FIP 1994). *Pitch Lake* (1996) was published by rempress. She has worked as a professional translator from Dutch to English, and is involved in the contemporary European poetry translation project of the CCCP. She lives in London.

'Photographs of the night-world taken by satellite show first world conurbations as dense light clusters dispersing into dotted patterns. The Western individual belongs, simply, to those spaces that are illuminated in the night-world and, like the universe, theoretically ever-expanding, until a new theory imagines its material differently. For various reasons, these lights keep me awake at night. Then, I read or write poems.'

Tracy Ryan Born in urban western Australia, settled in Britain in 1996. Worked as an editor, literature teacher, bookseller and librarian. Currently a temping secretary. Primary interests in learning languages and translating from French. Published works include the novel *Vamp* (Fremantle Art Centre Press 1997), who also publish *Killing Delilah* (1994) and *Bluebeard In Drag* (1996), *Slant* (rempress 1997) and *The Willing Eye* (Bloodaxe 1999).

'I am not committed to any one approach. Partly, I find out as I go along. Drawing on daily life, or dismantling and tinkering with other writing. Feminism and women writers have the biggest input. The political dimension is important, but I don't believe in making Simplistic connections between writing and world.'

Shelby Matthews Born in south England to Welsh parents with shades of Lancastrian. Trained as an economist. Has lived for some time amongst a flux of languages in Belgium and works there. *This which* in *New Tonal Language* (RSE, 2000) and the 3 works in *Foil* represent her debut publications.

'To write whatever is going on at the time. To catch myself in the gap between the lens of seeing and the lens of language. In whichever direction. Whereas the ground is solid but knowing it is porous. To have fun.'

However introduced to the Soles is a book, interlinking texts by three poets. For the purpose of *Foil* that entity has been retained. The authors are **Naill Quinn**, born in Ireland, currently completing 'a long poem whose form is determined by a confluence of chinese forms under the cloud of entropy.' **Nic Laight** was born on April 23rd in Bromsgrove, Worcestershire 1968. Published in H.I.T. and Angel Exhaust 15. Now retired. Poetic statement: No statement. No further work forthcoming. **Nick Macias**, b.London 1961 of Spanish Gibraltarian & Kentish apache educated in redistribution & Self preservation. Uncollected Poems Cornwall 1983 Began painting by instinct Summer 1990. Proprietor/chef on an Aberystwyth restaurant 1991-1997, which changed its name in Dec 1994 to yeskins, in tribute to Hank Yeskin (three more than ten) who actually wounded himself fighting the Devil. Wrote *Discovery* (1994), *However Introduced to the Soles* 1995 (U.N.K.N.). Put *Bluish Knight* together 1997, for the Soft Graceful delicate Soldier, (return, Caravan tour). 1999/2000 writing composites of ten fingered verse, to fill a book of home made paper.

This triumvirate was once based in Aberystwyth.

acknowledgements

Aaron Williamson *Cathedral Lung* (Creation 1991 (including *Freedom, Liberty & Tinsel* (Switch 1989)), *A Holythroat Symposium* (Creation 1993), *Cacaphonies* Gare du Nord 1998 and work from *Lives of Saints* Invisible Reader (Invisible Books 1995), Object Permanence, Big Allis (USA), plus 'Saint Gall','Saint Julian the Hospitaller', 'Saint Catherine dei Ricci' and 'Saint Valentine' first published here.

Meg Bateman *An Aghaidh na Siorraidheachd In the face of eternity* ed Christopher Whyte (Polygon 1991) *Aotromachd agus dàin eile / Lightness and other poems*, (Polygon 1997) *etruscan reader IX: Fred Beake, Nicholas Moore, Meg Bateman* (<u>etruscan</u>, 2000).

Khaled Hakim *H'm* (Short Run 1996), 'Letter to Antin' (Angel Exhaust 1997), 'letter to S' first published here.

Adrian Clarke *Obscure Disasters* (writers forum 1993).

Nicholas Johnson *Land, Selected Poems 1983-1998* (Mammon Press 1999), *Haul Song* (Mammon Press 1994, rev.1997), *Eel Earth* (writers forum 1993), 'Gillows Mohr' and 'layer's Text' first published here.

Caroline Bergvall *FLÈSH* is a version of *Flèsh A Coeur*, which was commissioned to be one part of *Volumes (of vulnerability)*, by Susan Johanknecht & Kate Meynell (Gefn Press: 2000).

Rajiv C Krishnan *The Watches* (Poetical Histories 1992) with acknowledgement to Peter Riley for the friends of Rajiv C.Krishnan.

Helen Macdonald *Safety Catch* (including *Simple Objects* (Poetical Histories 1993) in *etruscan reader I, Helen Macdonald, Gael Turnbull, Nicholas Johnson* (<u>etruscan</u> 1997), *Shaler's Fish* (<u>etruscan</u>, 2000).

Peter Manson *me generation* (writers forum 1997), *Summer Sadness* (Barque 1999) and 'Sarin Canasta' (First Offence 1998).

391

Rob MacKenzie *off Ardglas* (Invisible Books 1997), 'Comfort for Angus Smith' first published in *An Invisible reader* (Invisible Books 1995). 'air falbh' first published Form Books 1998. 'Taliban lamp-post' and 'Little Austrian Boy ...' first published here.

Alison Flett (some of the works first © Alison Kermack) *Restricted Vocabulary* (Clocktower 1991) *Writing Like A Bastard* (Rebel Inc., Rebel 100 series 1993, *Ahead of its time* (Jonathan Cape 1997/Vintage 1998), *cock* and *tail* used either side of a beer mat, project by Inverness Art Gallery.

Drew Milne 'A Statement on Purpose' (Angel Exhaust 1993), *Sheet Mettle* (Alfred David Editions 1994 (including *Satyrs and Mephitic Angels*, Equipage 1993)), *Bench Marks* (Alfred David Editions 1998).

John Kinsella *The Undertow*, New & Selected Poems (Arc 1996), *The Silo: A Pastoral Symphony* (Arc 1997), *Poems 1980-1994* (Fremantle Arts Centre, Press 1997/Bloodaxe 1998).

Aidan Andrew Dun *Vale Royal* (Goldmark 1995). 'India Canto, I', first published here.

Jennifer Chalmers *Peat* (Poetical Histories 1996).

Andrew Brewerton *Sirius* (Poetical Histories 1996).

John Cayley *Ink Bamboo* (Agenda/Bellew 1997). Two corresponding pages from *Oisleánd*, based on Nuala Ni Dhomhnaill's Oileán and an English version by John Cayley from John Montague's translation. The fade-out section of *Foil* is 'Pathways.'

Tertia Longmire *The Table Leaks its Object* (Magpie Press 1998) and 'Episodal inquiry gets bored quickly' first published here.

David Amery *Virtual Gardens*, privately printed 1998.

Ira Lightman *Loving Phase Transitions* (Sound & Language 1997), 'The Orchestration of Unhappiness', 'across the firmament, surface of doomed england' first published here.

Kevin Nolan *Alar* (Equipage 1997), *All Over Susan* (Barque 1998).

Danielle Hope *City Fox* (Rockingham Press 1997).

Harriet Tarlo *Brancepeth Beck* (The Other Press 1997), *Coast* first published here.

Brigid McLeer '*Collapsing Here, Version 2.3:* first published here *Home 'go fóil'* is a reconfigured version of a piece first published in Circa.

David Rees *The London* (Gratton Street Irregulars/West House Books 1997).

Tim Atkins *Folklore 1-25* (Heart Hammer 1995).

Richard A.Makin *fwd* (Equipage 1995) *too mouth for word* (Historical Research Limited Press 1996) and universelipre (equipage 1996). Work from *Ravine* first published here.

Karlien van den Beukel *Pitch Lake* (rem. press 1996) *Bathing Suites 1-5* (1-3 first published Angel Exhaust 1996) (*4-5* Big Allis).

Tracy Ryan *Slant* (rem.press 1997).

Shelby Matthews 'Een doodnormale vrouw', 'Body Flare', 'chat'ouille' first published here.

However Introduced to the Soles (Nick Macias), 'Song for Lucy' (Macias), 'One day experiment' (Nic Laight), 'osiris' (Niall Quinn), 'From Dostoievski wrung consection' (Quinn), 'The Wronged' (Laight), 'it was in the morning they took him' (Quinn), 'man' (Laight) and 'ten' (Quinn).

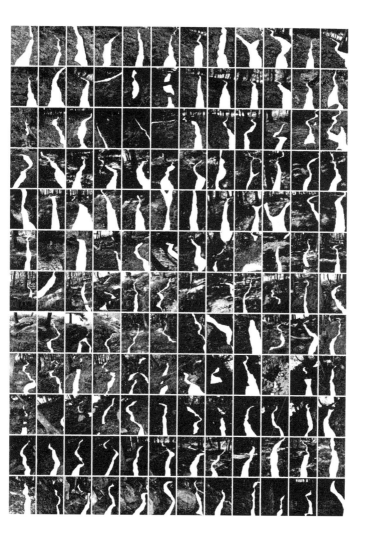

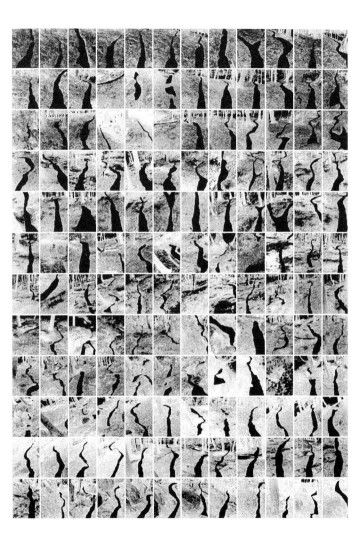